ON FREEDOM

BOSTON UNIVERSITY STUDIES IN PHILOSOPHY AND RELIGION

General Editor: Leroy S. Rouner

Volume Ten

Volume Nine
Human Rights and the World's Religions

Volume Eight
Civil Religion and Political Theology

Volume Seven
Knowing Religiously

Volume Six
On Nature

Volume Five
Religious Pluralism

Volume Four
Foundations of Ethics

Volume Three
Meaning, Truth, and God

Volume Two
Transcendence and the Sacred

Volume One
Myth, Symbol, and Reality

On Freedom

Edited by
Leroy S. Rouner

UNIVERSITY OF NOTRE DAME PRESS
Notre Dame, Indiana

Copyright © 1989 by
University of Notre Dame Press
Notre Dame, Indiana 46556
All Rights Reserved

Library of Congress Cataloging-in-Publication Data

On freedom / edited by Leroy S. Rouner.
    p. cm. — (Boston University studies in philosophy and religion ; v. 10)
  Includes indexes.
   ISBN 978-0-268-03709-3
  1. Freedom (Theology) 2. Liberty. I. Rouner, Leroy S. II. Series.
BT810.2.O5 1989
123'.5—dc20   89-33164

Contents

Preface — vii

Acknowledgments — x

Contributors — xi

Introduction • *Leroy S. Rouner* — 1

PART I: THEOLOGIES OF FREEDOM

1. Incarnation and Determinate Freedom
   • *Nicholas Lash* — 15

2. Is Protestantism the "Religion of Freedom"?
   • *Jürgen Moltmann* — 30

3. Freedom, the Self, and the Other
   • *David W. Tracy* — 46

4. Freedom, Tolerance, and Puritan Commitment
   • *Robert C. Neville* — 59

PART II: PHILOSOPHIES OF FREEDOM

5. Freedom as Self-Determination • *John E. Smith* — 79

6. Freedom and the State • *Frithjof Bergmann* — 96

7. Science, Theology, and Freedom: A New Look at the Galileo Case • *James R. Langford* — 108

8. Freedom as Action in Indian Philosophy
   • *J. N. Mohanty* — 126

PART III: FREEDOM IN SOCIETY

9. Social Structures and Structural Ethics
   • *Louis Dupré*   143
10. Evading the Shadows: Freedom and the Social World • *Ruth L. Smith*   163
11. Mass Death and Autonomous Selves
    • *Edith Wyschogrod*   180

Author Index   197

Subject Index   199

Preface

Boston University Studies in Philosophy and Religion is a joint project of the Boston University Institute for Philosophy and Religion and the University of Notre Dame Press. The essays in each annual volume are edited from the previous year's lecture program of the Institute. The Director of the Institute, who also serves as editor of these Studies, chooses a theme and invites participants to lecture at Boston University in the course of the academic year. The papers are then revised by their authors, and the editor selects and edits the essays to be included in these Studies. In preparation is Volume Eleven, *On Peace*.

The Boston University Institute for Philosophy and Religion is a Center of the Graduate School, and is sponsored jointly by the Department of Philosophy, the Department of Religion, and the School of Theology. The Institute is made possible by regular financial support from the Graduate School. The Institute is an interdisciplinary and ecumenical forum. Within the academic community it is committed to open interchange on fundamental issues in philosophy and religious study which transcend the narrow specializations of academic curricula. Outside the University it seeks to recover the public tradition of philosophical discourse which was a lively part of American intellectual life in the early years of this century before the professionalization of both philosophy and religious reflection. At a time when too much academic writing is incomprehensible, or irrelevant, or both, we try to present readable essays by acknowledged authorities on critical human issues.

FOR RAIMUNDO PANIKKAR

whose scholarship and cultural empathy embrace both India and the West. His Institute lectures have been models of elegant philosophical insight, enlivened by a passionate heart.

Acknowledgments

Our authors, as always, deserve our primary thanks. Several of them came from great distances to participate in our program, and we are grateful to them all for their help.

Barbara Darling-Smith has managed to finish her Ph.D., teach courses at neighboring colleges, and still maintain her good cheer while administering the Institute program, and turning out another flawlessly copy-edited manuscript. Her work on this book has been simply invaluable.

Greg Rockwell has overseen the production process for the University of Notre Dame Press, and Editor Ann Rice has once more expedited publication with her quiet professionalism and personal grace.

A tenth volume is something of an anniversary, and we celebrate it by welcoming Jim Langford, Director of the Press, as one of our authors. He continues to be a major source of ideas and encouragement for this series, and we cherish him as a colleague and a friend.

Contributors

FRITHJOF BERGMANN has been Professor of Philosophy at the University of Michigan since 1973. He is also Director of the Center for New Work in Flint and has acted as consultant to the National Endowment for the Humanities, the National Humanities Faculty, the Bendix Corporation, the Xerox Corporation, and the McDonald's Corporation. His book *On Being Free*, first published in 1973, is in its twelfth printing. In addition to numerous philosophical articles, he has also produced several philosophy videotapes. Professor Bergmann received his "Matura" degree at the Realgymnasium Gmunden in Austria, his B.A. in philosophy at Lewis and Clark College, and his Ph.D. in philosophy at Princeton University.

LOUIS DUPRÉ was born in Belgium and graduated from the University of Louvain. His doctoral dissertation on *The Starting Point of Marxist Philosophy* was published with a government grant and in 1956 received the biennial J. M. Huyghe prize in social studies. In 1956 he received a study grant from the Danish government to do research on Kierkegaard at the Royal Library in Copenhagen. In 1958 he emigrated to the United States and taught philosophy at Georgetown University until 1972. In 1973 he was appointed T. Lawrason Riggs Professor in the Philosophy of Religion at Yale University. Among his most recent books are *Marx's Social Critique of Culture; The Deeper Life; A Dubious Heritage; Transcendent Selfhood;* and *The Other Dimension*.

JAMES R. LANGFORD is Director of the University of Notre Dame Press. He was educated by the Dominicans at the Aquinas Institute, where he received both the Ph.Lic. and S.T.L. degrees. He taught at the University of Michigan and the University of Notre Dame and is author of *Galileo, Science, and the Church* (1971). He has also written numerous articles and reviews in the field of Galileo studies. Prior to assuming directorship of the University of Notre Dame Press in 1974, he was Executive Editor of the University of Michigan Press for five years; before that he was editor at Doubleday.

NICHOLAS LASH is Norris-Hulse Professor of Divinity in the University of Cambridge, and also a Fellow of Clare Hall. A member of the central directorate of *Concilium*, he also serves on the Theology Committee of the Roman Catholic Episcopal Conference of England and Wales. His books include *Theology on the Way to Emmaus; A Matter of Hope: A Theologian's Reflections on the Thought of Karl Marx; Theology on Dover Beach;* and *Voices of Authority*. Most recently he has published *Easter in Ordinary: Reflections on Human Experience and the Knowledge of God*, his 1986 Richard Lectures at the University of Virginia.

J. N. MOHANTY was educated at Calcutta University (B.A., 1947; M.A., 1949) and Göttingen University (Ph.D., 1954). He has been Vivekānanda Professor of Philosophy at the University of Bevawan, India (1962–67); Acharya B. N. Seal Professor of Mental and Moral Science at the University of Calcutta (1967–72); Professor of Philosophy at the New School for Social Research, New York (1973–78); and George L. Cross Research Professor at the University of Oklahoma (1978–85). Since 1985 he has been Professor of Philosophy at Temple University. He has been president of the Indian Philosophical Congress and Visiting Fellow at All Souls College, Oxford. His most recent publications are *Husserl and Frege* and *The Possibility of Transcendental Philosophy*.

JÜRGEN MOLTMANN was educated at the University of Göttingen where he received his Ph.D. in 1955 and his Habilitation in 1957. He is also the recipient of several honorary degrees and the Elba Library Prize. He is Professor of Systematic Theology at the University of Tübingen. Among his many books are *On Human Dignity: Political Theology and Ethics; The Trinity and the Kingdom; The Future of Creation; The Church in the Power of the Spirit; The Crucified God; Religion, Revolution, and the Future;* and *Theology of Hope.*

ROBERT C. NEVILLE received his B.A., M.A., and Ph.D. at Yale University. He is Dean of the School of Theology at Boston University, and also Director of the Division of Religious and Theological Studies and Professor of Philosophy, Religion, and Theology there. Prior to coming to Boston University in 1987 he taught at the State University of New York at Stony Brook. He has written numerous articles and books, among them *The Puritan Smile; The Tao and the Daimon; Reconstruction of Thinking; Creativity and God; Soldier, Sage, Saint;* and *The Cosmology of Freedom.*

LEROY S. ROUNER is Professor of Philosophy, Religion, and Philosophical Theology at Boston University, Director of the Institute for Philosophy and Religion, and General Editor of this Series. He did his Ph.D. with John Herman Randall, Jr., at Columbia University on the philosophy of William Ernest Hocking, and is the author of *Within Human Experience: The Philosophy of William Ernest Hocking;* editor and co-author of the Hocking *Festschrift, Philosophy, Religion and the Coming World Civilization;* and, with John Howie, of *The Wisdom of William Ernest Hocking.* He taught for five years in Bangalore, India, and drove his family overland by Land Rover from India to England in 1966–67. He has been Visiting Professor at the University of Hawaii. His works in press are *Civil Religion, Human Community, and the Christian Hope;* and a memoir, *The Long Way Home.*

JOHN E. SMITH is Clark Professor of Philosophy at Yale University. He has also taught at Santa Clara University, Barnard College, and Vassar College. He has delivered numerous public lectures, including the Cardozo Lecture at the City University of New York, the Hoover Lectures at the University of Chicago, and the Dudleian Lectures at Harvard, and he has also been invited panelist at the Columbia University Seminars on the Media. Among his books are: *The Spirit of American Philosophy; Royce's Social Infinite; The Challenge of Religion; Reason and God;* and *Value Convictions and Higher Education.* Professor Smith received his A.B. at Columbia College, his B.D. at Union Theological Seminary, and his Ph.D. at Columbia University.

RUTH L. SMITH received her Ph.D. in social ethics at Boston University, where she was a Roothbert Fellow. She also holds an M.T.S. in ethics and theology from Harvard Divinity School, an M.A. in linguistics from Ohio University, and a B.A. in literature and music from East Tennessee State University. Currently Assistant Professor in the Humanities at Worcester Polytechnic Institute, she has also taught at Ohio Wesleyan University and Andover Newton Theological School. The author of numerous articles, she is presently working on a book on Reinhold Niebuhr and liberalism to be published by the Edwin Mellen Press. Professor Smith is also serving as consultant to the Global Village Documentary Film Company in the making of a Public Broadcasting Service film on "The Value of Life."

DAVID W. TRACY is Distinguished Service Professor and on the Committee of Ideas and Methods at the University of Chicago, where he has taught since 1969. He has also taught at Yale University, Catholic University of America, the North American College in Rome, and Loyola University. He co-edits the *Journal of Religion* and is on the editorial boards of various publications, including the *Journal of Pastoral Psychology, Concilium,* and *Theology Today.* He is the author of several books, among them *Bernard Lonergan's Interpretation of the Exigence in St. Thomas Aquinas; The Achievement of Bernard Lonergan: The New Pluralism in Theology; A Blessed Rage for Order;* and *The Analytical Imagination.* His latest book is *Plurality and Ambiguity.*

EDITH WYSCHOGROD received her A.B. from Hunter College and her Ph.D. from Columbia University. She has been Professor of Philosophy at Queens College of the City University of New York since 1981 and has also taught at the State University of New York at Stony Brook. In 1987–88 she was recipient of a Woodrow Wilson Fellowship to write a book-length study: *The Exemplary Individual: Towards a Phenomenological Ethics.* Her other books are *Spirit in Ashes: Hegel, Heidegger and Man-Made Mass Death; Emmanuel Levinas: The Problem of Ethical Metaphysics;* and *The Phenomenon of Death: Faces of Mortality.*

Introduction

LEROY S. ROUNER

FREEDOM IS A BEDROCK conviction of the modern Western mind, and for Americans it virtually defines a way of life. America is "the land of the free," and the most compelling rationale for moral choices, both political and personal, is the defense of freedom. So Roosevelt's "Four Freedoms" rallied the nation in the Second World War, and "freedom of choice" is a critical principle in the current abortion debate.

Liberalism gave the amorphous belief in freedom philosophic shape, grounding it in the notion of autonomous selfhood. Because the self becomes itself through acts of will, it must be free to act, and therefore autonomous. Liberalism was never clear exactly how autonomous individuals were joined together for the common weal, but as long as there was "a common cake of custom," derived from the religious and moral values of Christendom, this weakness in liberalism's logic was not troubling. Liberalism celebrated individual creativity, freed from constraint by either church or state, and could point proudly to great achievements in science, government, and the arts which various cultural freedoms had enabled.

The essays which follow explore several broad questions which surfaced when our economic, political, and cultural life became both pluralized and globalized. It has become increasingly apparent that free acts of individual wills, in and of themselves, are irrelevant both to the creative opportunities of world community, and to the destructive possibilities of atomic holocaust and ecological disaster. How are we to understand freedom in this new situation?

Our first question concerns the relation of Christian thought to freedom in a post-Christian age. If secular liberalism had indeed drawn moral and spiritual capital from Christendom, can contemporary Christian thought continue to contribute to a new world which is both post-Christian and postliberal? Can freedom remain vital if cut off entirely from its religious roots? These issues are addressed in our first section on "Theologies of Freedom."

The second question focuses on philosophical reconstructions of the idea of freedom. To what extent can we adapt the liberal view of the autonomous self to the requirements of community action in a global crisis, and how will that reconstructed idea of freedom relate individuals to the state? What can we learn from the past about conflicts between scientific freedom and religious authority? And how may non-Western notions of freedom be understood, if not appropriated, in order to make global community action coherent? These themes run through the essays in Part II, "Philosophies of Freedom."

Finally, in Part III, "Freedom in Society," we explore the possibility that individual selves are no more autonomous than they are social. What can we learn about the freedom of the self from contemporary social philosophies like Marxism and feminism, and the unprecedented contemporary phenomenon of manmade mass death? If the liberal idea of the autonomous self required a "society," structured by a contract among individuals, can a more social conception of selfhood lead toward a "community," in which individuals can find a larger part of their identity as selves?

We begin with Nicholas Lash's essay on "Incarnation and Determinate Freedom" in which he notes that our Western obsession with freedom began in dignity, because its source was in our likeness to God. This dignity was maintained when freedom became a rejection of all absolutes, and the celebration of new powers won through our autonomy. Under the pressure of much contemporary suffering and disillusionment, however, the freedom of the autonomous individual has been reduced to desperate plight. Lash traces this development historically, from Descartes to Sartre, noting that the "disappearance of God" is everywhere confidently proclaimed even as virtually every contemporary culture continues to be "*awash with religion.*"

While challenging some superficialities in the secularist presupposition, Lash is primarily concerned with a Christian understanding of what it means to be adult in our contemporary situation. Secularists assume that "the absolute" is the primary concern of religious faith, but Lash argues that the task of adulthood is the choice of finitude before God. "Adulthood, thus construed, would be a matter of discovering that it is possible, without diminution of dignity, abdication of rationality, or loss of freedom, to yield to what we know and be commanded by it."

Religious maturity, he suggests, is learning to worship, but not worshipping either oneself or any other thing. It is in such worship that modern autonomy is transcended, and our God-focus redirected to "the form and flesh of God's appearing" in the Incarnation. Lash emphasizes the conviction that our bodies and our finite condition are our home, and that current flights from finitude, into feeling or thought, are rejections of our human freedom. The Incarnate God of Christianity rescues freedom from the lonely plight of secular autonomy.

Jürgen Moltmann focuses specifically on Protestantism's contribution. He, too, notes the malaise in modern notions of freedom, brought on by our realization that freedom requires a responsibility which we are no longer willing to bear. He also touches on the theme of adulthood when he asks, "Do we really want to grow up, or are we longing for a child's religious tutelage from 'Mother Church' or 'Father State' or 'Daddy *Guru*'?" He outlines three formative epochs for the Protestant conception of freedom: 1) the Reformation in the sixteenth century; 2) the Enlightenment in the eighteenth century; and 3) the ecumenism of the twentieth century. He argues that the Reformation was concerned with the "religion of the faith"; that the Enlightenment was concerned with the "religion of freedom"; and that the ecumenism of our own day focuses on the "religion of the community."

After summarizing the characteristic features of the Reformation and the Enlightenment, Moltmann outlines the "religion of community." It involves living ecumenically. "Ecumenical community," he suggests, "arises everywhere in the world where we find ourselves under Christ's cross as brothers and sisters, as hungry people in common poverty." Living ecumenically then leads to thinking ecumenically, in which particularism is overcome and the narrowness of traditional horizons broadened. This leads to a new understanding of freedom, which derives, not from choice or the language of dominion, but from the language of community where freedom means the same as friendship. We can be free,

Moltmann says, only where we can be ourselves, and we can be ourselves only where we are known and appreciated and accepted as we are. Through discovery of the transnational and transconfessional catholicity of the Church, ecumenical Protestantism prepares the Christian community to "enter the age of humanity's world history."

In "Freedom, the Self, and the Other" David Tracy also notes the deprivatizing of both Catholic and Protestant theologies, and the emergence of new theories of the self and its freedom. He proposes a thought experiment in which he asks: "Can one affirm a basic, even communal, Christian scriptural understanding of the self as free agent before God and then see what light that rhetoric of the self may cast on one great alternative contemporary reading?" The alternative contemporary reading Tracy has in mind is Jacques Lacan's reading of Freud. Here Tracy, the American Catholic, Lash, the British Protestant, and Moltmann, the German Protestant, all formulate their theological notion of freedom in remarkably similar ways, thus lending some modest support for Moltmann's observations on ecumenicity.

Tracy summarizes the main Christian confession: "We believe in Jesus the Christ with the apostles." In the Christian narrative which embodies this confession he finds disclosed a self with freedom to respond to God and to others through the power of this Jesus. This freedom is not monolithic, but a constant interplay between a prophetic reading which emphasizes freedom as responsible agency, and a mystical reading which emphasizes freedom as love. Tracy's formulation is not unlike Moltmann's notion of freedom as both ecumenical outreach and simple friendship. For Tracy, then, freedom is the activity of a self-as-agent-in-process, and not an isolated "ego."

With this analysis in hand he turns to the Lacan interpretation of Freud, noting that Freud was a prophet whose rhetoric was also interrupted — as in the Christian interruption of the prophet by the mystic — by what Tracy calls "the voice of the Other." His suggestion is that categories of Christian thought about freedom do illuminate Lacan's reading of Freud, but that the debate between prophets and mystics, whether Christian or secular, continue to engage the Other's freedom with that of the self-in-process.

Our first section on theologies of freedom concludes with

Robert Neville's essay on "Freedom, Tolerance, and Puritan Commitment." He begins boldly with the "principle of universal public responsibility," which clearly presupposes something other than the classical liberal notion of the autonomous self in holding that "everyone in a social group is regularly responsible for all the group's public obligations." He credits this principle to Puritanism, contrasting it to the liberal view that personal responsibility derives from the social contract, and that one has no public responsibility apart from the contract.

Neville's concerns are these: What are the social implications of this principle? What kind of social commitment is required to exercise universal responsibility? How can that commitment be exercised without interfering in the rights of others? And is there a genuine sense of freedom native to universal public responsibility?

In contrast to liberal notions of atomic individualism, Neville argues that people gain individuality through fulfilling their connections with the things that have normative bearing on their lives. He implies that community precedes individuality in the order of things. "Individuation through commitment" thus becomes a corollary of the principle of universal public responsibility. But tolerance is required to prevent each responsible self from making others fulfill their responsibility as one sees it. Here liberalism and Puritanism join hands in the affirmation that each person is the responsible author of his or her actions. "The seat of responsibility is in the individual subject, just as the content of responsibility is in the objective goods that are obligatory to serve."

Neville concludes that freedom is possible in this context, and outlines his case for four freedoms: political, personal, social, and spiritual. Political freedom recognizes the individual's claim on authorship and responsibility. Personal freedom is the freedom to act, to choose among alternatives, to choose according to standards, and to criticize standards. Social freedom includes opportunity, social pluralism, integral social life, and political participation. Spiritual freedom is concerned with "the attainment of spiritual excellence or perfection," a note from Neville's Methodist heritage, not heard from his Catholic and Calvinist predecessors in this discussion.

Part II, "Philosophies of Freedom," begins with John Smith's essay on "Freedom as Self-Determination." After preliminary considerations concerning determinism and possibility, without which a doctrine of freedom is impossible, he turns directly to the nature of that self which, as agent, exercises freedom. Whereas our theological authors were largely concerned with connecting selfhood to a social world, Smith is concerned to analyze selfhood from within. He rejects the notion, implied in the liberal view of the self as autonomous, that selfhood is grounded in some prior essence which merely unfolds in time. The self, he tells us, desires, hopes, believes, wills, and so forth, so that it is not to be thought of as "all there" in any given moment, since the self is what it hopes for and desires, as well as what it has accomplished. Selfhood, for Smith, is a task and an achievement, even though there must be an incipient form of selfhood as a precondition for becoming a fully developed self. This incipient self is neither a substance nor a collection of episodes; it is the dominant purpose which creates a meaningful biography expressing what that person means to be and to become.

The self is therefore not only its career; it is also its will and character, and Smith's doctrine of freedom hinges on a proper understanding of these two ideas. In willing there are four features: preference, our capacity to evaluate goals; purpose, what we mean to do and be; power, our effort of accomplishment; and perseverance, which forges and sustains character. The character of a self is analogous to the nature of an object, but the nature of an object is given, whereas the character of a self is achieved through perseverance in expressing our purpose. Freedom, for Smith, is the possibility of failure in that character making, as well as the possibility of success.

Smith concludes his argument with three illustrations of perseverance from the lives of Socrates, Antigone, and Martin Luther. In each case concrete action was called for which reaffirmed the purposes of that self, making her or him whole, and in so doing exercising freedom as self-determination.

Frithjof Bergmann's essay on "Freedom and the State" begins with a criticism of the popular American notion of freedom as unfetteredness. The cowboy and the convict are our symbols of the free and the unfree. But freedom as the absence of obstacles is not a sustainable idea, as he readily shows, and a government based on such a concept of freedom would be impossible, even unimaginable. The "obstacle-free" view of freedom has created calamity in both family life and education, but the idea continues to inform the popular view that "the government which governs best is the government which governs least."

Bergmann's argument is that, while this proposition has an air of self-evidence about it, it is patently false, and seems reasonable only because the presuppositions of "obstacle thinking" equate less government with more freedom. Americans, he notes, are predisposed to think of the state as curtailing freedom. His argument is diametrically opposed to the "obstacle thinker's" view of the state. Bergmann proposes that more government can mean more freedom. For example, "The state can impose limitations on everyone, but on balance these reduce for everyone the obstacles they face, and the result is thus greater (real) freedom."

He notes that those conservatives who are most in favor of less government actually also favor more government in areas of their own self-interest, such as "law and order," or the control of objectionable literature, or the raising of protectionist tariffs. He also counters the view that more government means less efficiency by pointing to examples of large-scale government efficiency in places as diverse as Germany and Mexico, and to the "pratfalls" of those American corporations which supposedly embody the efficient virtues credited to private enterprise. He concludes that the philosophical issues raised by obstacle thinking in the conservative-liberal debate have so obscured the real issues as to require new concepts in order for discussions of political philosophy in America to be fruitful once again.

James Langford's essay on "Science, Theology and Freedom" is a case study of the social conflict between scientific freedom and religious authority. The case is the famous trial of Galileo and Langford approaches it cautiously, reminding us that with all the wealth of historical material now available to us, "we know enough to be aware that simplified causal explanations do not suffice" and that "chance and circumstance played more than bit parts in the drama." He approaches his task systematically, beginning with what happened, then trying to understand why it happened and whether it could have been avoided. Finally he asks what lessons from the case are relevant today.

In telling the Galileo story Langford dwells at length on a

book by Campanella written in 1615. Campanella defended Galileo's right to philosophize on cosmological issues because he wanted to see a Christian-authored philosophy develop. It seemed absurd to Campanella that the church should condemn the Christian Galileo in favor of the pagan Aristotle. Campanella not only warned against a too literal interpretation of the relevant scriptural texts, he also pointed out that the message of the Bible is religious, not scientific, and quoted Augustine in defense of his view that philosophical theories are not to be criticized or defended as though they were doctrines of faith.

Langford notes that there would have been no Galileo case had Campanella's extensive work been taken seriously. Langford's conclusion is carefully drawn. He is persuaded that Campanella has provided a workable solution for all apparent discrepancies between Scripture and science, and that a little more goodwill and open-mindedness could have saved the day. He notes with distress the contemporary silencing of Latin American liberation theologians by Rome, and the removal of influential European and American Catholic theologians from teaching positions. Rome is "still unwilling to respond to doctrinal differences by careful and measured argumentation rather than authoritative confrontation." He concludes that there is yet much to be learned from the Galileo case.

With J. N. Mohanty's essay on "Freedom as Action in Indian Philosophy" we gain comparative perspective on our topic, and insight into the distinctively transcendental nature of Hindu doctrines of freedom.

He begins by analyzing action in terms of the agent, the knowledge or desire to act, and effort of action. The agent is independent since he or she possesses will, which is conducive to action. Knowledge concerns knowing that something is to be done, that it can be done, and that some good will come from doing it. The powers of the self as agent are therefore cognition, desire, volition, and effort. These powers are not entirely unlike those enumerated by Smith in his analysis of willing, but Mohanty points out that the Hindu categories do not necessarily imply a doctrine of freedom at this level, since knowledge that I can do something is balanced by the determining causal power of the knowledge that the goal is good. In clear distinction to Smith's view, Hindu philosophy argues that we do not choose the goal; the goodness of the goal "chooses" us. So Mohanty is initially ambivalent about whether or not Hindu philosophers had an operational doctrine of "worldly" freedom, especially since Hindu and Buddhist philosophers did not use the same tripartite faculty psychology which undergirds much Western philosophy of the will. Mohanty then turns to the Hindu notion of *karma*, wherein all actions lead to either pleasure or pain. *Karma* is not deterministic, however, since it is one's own past actions in previous lives which determine one's present condition, and one's present choices which will determine one's future. But *karma* for the moral agent takes place in the context of *dharma*, which is a form of moral law. Mohanty compares it to Hegel's *Sittlichkeit*, the law of a natural community like the Greek *polis*, where everyone knew what they were supposed to do. Finally he explores the notion of *mokṣa* — a form of transcendental freedom, a state of being "consequent on knowing the truth," which transcends *dharma*. Mohanty makes it clear that there is no direct transition from *dharma* to *mokṣa* in Hindu thought, and that the freedom of *mokṣa* transcends any moral law. This liberated person "follows only that *dharma* which is consistent with (ultimate) self-knowledge, and practices it with inner spontaneity — not as following rules."

Louis Dupré's "Social Structures and Structural Ethics" is a brief history of ethical theory in the West. His philosophical focus is on the relation between individual and public morality, and his concern for an ethics of community, the "bonum commune," is close to the one Robert Neville voiced in proposing his principle of universal public responsibility. Dupré sees a sharp break between the classical ethics of the Aristotelian, Stoic, and Scholastic traditions on the one hand, and the ethics characteristic of the modern nation-state on the other. Whereas the earlier tradition found a coherent way to integrate public and private morality, the era of the modern nation-state reduces morality to the private sphere and introduces *Realpolitik* as the appropriate basis for political action.

For Aristotle, the moral virtues of the individual were precisely those intended to "achieve and promote the good of the community." "To abide only by the strict personal obligations of distributive justice would not fulfill the demands of *ethics* in that higher sense in which Aristotle understood the term." The philosophical underpinning of this view was the social conception of nature as both "first things" and "the essential character of a thing." So for Plato the *polis* of the *Republic* is "the best city, the city according to nature." In the Aristotelian development of this community ethic "what is good" is not derived from some angelic point of view but reflects the reasoning of a community in which the common good "naturally" lends meaning to the good for each individual.

With the rise of the nation-state, however, the decision of the sovereign, as articulated in the theory of divine right, is ultimately arbitrary, not relying on any intrinsic rationality in the social order. So society becomes a voluntary association rather than a natural one. Dupré's conclusion is somber. Today we face critical problems of interrelationship among nation-states with no common notion of a common good to guide us.

In "Evading the Shadows: Freedom and the Social World" Ruth Smith joins those who are concerned to analyze liberalism in order to deconstruct its formal and naturalistic claims. In focusing on the relationship between freedom and the social world she seeks to dislodge "the imperial claims of the autonomous self as the seat of freedom" and in so doing introduce new questions about the nature of the social world. Her criticism of the autonomous self is that its claim to universality requires that it remove all elements of contingency and dependency from its self-understanding and identify them with the "other." The autonomous self thus becomes "free" at the expense of all that is "other." Smith points out that this view does not take the self's own contingency seriously, and by making the other "more contingent, more socially embedded, and less free" delegitimizes the other as a source of social and moral power. People who are thus "outside the canons of autonomy in their lack of economic or political or cultural power" are trivialized.

In her analysis of contingency as the opposite of freedom she notes that we fear contingency as the imperfect and insufficient, but also as that which is social and located, and she comments, "In fearing our shadow, we also fear ourselves, ourselves who are free of location and so can only be critical." Smith counters this Western mistrust of the contingent with the deconstructionist argument that the identity of selves is not given but arises out of the play of self-sameness with otherness or alterity. In this view she comes close to elements of David Tracy's view of the self-in-process and John Smith's view of the self as an unfinished project.

Smith concludes that the autonomous self, in removing otherness from itself, is committed to a critical stance toward a world which it does not seem to need. It therefore lacks any basis for understanding the other and fails to grasp its need for the other as necessary for its own becoming.

We conclude with Edith Wyschogrod's "Mass Death and Autonomous Selves." Like so many of our other authors, she too is critical of the idea of the self as independent thinker and actor. Like Bergmann, Wyschogrod is less concerned with the philosophical concept of the autonomous self as articulated in the history of philosophy than she is with the role it plays in our current common-sense view. In the first part of her essay she describes two characteristic forms of manmade mass death: the concentration camp and nuclear war. In the second section of her essay she turns to various models of the self, emphasizing the sea change that has taken place in Western philosophy as a result of manmade mass death, especially in regard to agency.

Wyschogrod notes that earlier Western views of selfhood have all interpreted the self as a substantive entity of some sort which has thoughts, intentions, desires, habits, and the like. This self is the subject of cognitive, productive, and moral acts. She is sympathetic with those who see the self as relational, but admits that pure relationality undermines the individual boundedness of each self. She turns to Heidegger, who argues that "what makes selves individuals is the relation of each self to its own death." This is rather different from John Smith's view that a self is defined by relation to its own purposes. But if one takes death as self-definitive, then the experience of manmade mass death will radically alter self-conception.

She argues that the death-world of the concentration camp and nuclear war both diminish the agent's capacity to affect future events. The threat of nuclear war limits the freedom of all individuals, so a limited benevolence is called for since "the transactional social self that desires to persevere in existence includes a relational field of others in its wish. Once the whole human community is threatened, the self must wish for the survival of everyone in wishing for the preservation of a few."

Our authors are virtually all agreed in reshaping the idea of the self in a direction which is more social and relational. As a result the notion of freedom becomes less clear. While the autonomous self will no longer do, its freedom was at least clearly stated. The current instinct for community waits for further fashioning of a doctrine of freedom which can do justice to the creative purposes of the individual and somehow integrate them with a sense of the common good. That project will be the focus of Volume 12 in this series, *On Community*.

PART I

Theologies of Freedom

1
Incarnation and Determinate Freedom
NICHOLAS LASH

FROM DIGNITY TO PLIGHT

THE OBSESSION WITH FREEDOM is a defining feature of the modern Western mind. Even though freedom has not always been the keynote of political action and moral argument, men and women everywhere have sought and celebrated such freedom as lay within their vision and their reach.

It is the correlation between our freedom and the being and action of God which especially interests me. And on this topic, the dominant ethos in modern Western thought has undergone a series of most interesting modulations.[1] From the *locus* of our likeness to God, freedom became, first, the goal of our struggle against all absolutes, then the celebration of autonomy won and power displayed, then, gradually, under the pressure of much suffering and disillusionment, something much more modest, more stoical. Finally, in terror, freedom becomes our plight.[2]

In the beginning of modernity was the will. "It is a supreme perfection in man that he acts voluntarily, that is, freely; this makes him in a special way the author of his actions and deserving of praise for what he does." Thus Descartes, for whom the nature of the will and its freedom is the point of our *resemblance* to God. As constituted by God we are, like God, the authors of our acts. Freedom is our godlike dignity.[3]

That was 1644. Move on two hundred years, through Enlightenment and the bourgeois revolutions, to the Paris Manuscripts of 1844: "A *being* sees himself as independent only when he stands on his own feet, and he only stands on his own feet when he owes his *existence* to himself. A man who lives by the grace of another regards himself as a dependent being." Human freedom, no longer our likeness to God, is now the principle of our antagonism to divine sovereignty. As Marx had put it the previous year, the question as to whether sovereignty resided in the people or in the monarch was liable to obscure the fact that we are here dealing with "two *wholly opposed conceptions of sovereignty*, of which one can come into being only in the *monarch* and the other only in the *people*. It is analogous to the question, whether God or man is sovereign. One of the two must be false."[4]

By the end of the century, the battle was over. Prometheus stood lord and master of his world, unchallenged and unchecked. But already the *hubris* is set in counterpoint to darker tones. To be unchallenged is, after all, to be alone. Listen to William James, in 1904:

> From the fact that finite experiences must draw support from one another, philosophers pass to the notion that experience *überhaupt* must need an absolute support. The denial of such a notion by humanism lies probably at the root of most of the dislike which it incurs. But is this not the globe, the elephant, and the tortoise all over again? Must not something end by supporting itself? Humanism is willing to let finite experience be self-supporting. Somewhere being must immediately breast nonentity. Why may not the advancing front of experience, carrying its immanent satisfactions and dissatisfactions, cut against the black inane as the luminous orb of the moon cuts the cerulean abyss?[5]

James's imagery, of ship prow and moonlight, suggests that solitude be borne in courage and tranquillity. And yet, as Craig remarks, for many this imagery will invoke "as terrifying a feeling of the trackless void surrounding human life as anything ever produced by any purveyor of existentialist *Angst*." Hence the slogan which Craig proposes for the twentieth-century *Weltbild* of freedom as predicament is that of the "Agent in the Void."[6]

In James, the terror is latent. Ever the patrician, he whistles stoically in the dark. In Sartre, however, as in many subsequent writers, the implications of the radically self-constitutive character of human freedom have been thought through without ambiguity: "For human reality, to be is to *choose oneself;* nothing comes to it either from the outside or from within which it can *receive or accept.* Without any help whatsoever, it is entirely abandoned to the intolerable necessity of making itself be — down to the slightest detail."[7]

"Intolerable necessity"— one need not be an existentialist to feel the cold wind that blows across the consequences of the choices we have made, across the wilderness of wartime Poland, Ethiopia, Japan, and the differently devastated forests of Brazil and Vietnam.

Listen to one more voice:

> Mankind loses religion as it moves through history, but the loss leaves its mark behind. Part of the drives and desires which religious belief preserved and kept alive are detached from the inhibiting religious form and become productive forces in social practice. In the process even the immoderation characteristic of shattered illusions acquires a positive form and is truly transformed. In a really free mind the concept of infinity is preserved in an awareness of the finality of human life and of the unalterable aloneness of men, and it keeps society from indulging in a thoughtless optimism, an inflation of its own knowledge into a new religion.[8]

Max Horkheimer detested "the fetishist handling of categories" in *Being and Nothingness,* in consequence of which "the dialectical finesse and complexity of thought has been turned into a glittering machinery of metal. Words like *l'être en soi* and *l'être pour soi* function as kinds of pistons."[9] This may be overstating it, but the asceticism of his own account of freedom as protective, in acknowledgment of finitude and aloneness, of the echoes of infinity, is in sober contrast to the destructive, self-indulgent exuberance of both Promethean optimism and Sartrean despair.

The modern moods of freedom do not fall into any simple chronological pattern, for two reasons. First, even the darkest accents of freedom as predicament were already sounded by Nietzsche. Secondly, as new moods emerge from changing circumstances, old ones seldom simply fade away. There are "contemporaries" alive today not only of Sartre and Horkheimer, but also of James, Marx, and even Descartes.

THE DISAPPEARANCE OF GOD

Read as straightforward description of our circumstances, Sartre's characterization of human reality seems simply false. We can and do receive and accept all manner of things from outside our individual selves: things such as language and identity, shelter and suffering, pain and delight, gratitude and disease. The self-constituting individual is a fiction of the modern imagination.

Not that the fiction lacks sense. False as empirical description, it may with hideous accuracy portray our moral condition. "What this man lacked," says Stanley Cavell of Othello, "was not certainty. He knew everything, but he could not yield to what he knew, be commanded by it."[10] To yield, to be commanded, to receive, to accept: fragile and fraught with danger, pregnant with slavery and betrayal, though concession, obedience, reception, and acceptance may be, they are yet the hallmarks of both infancy and adulthood. Between them comes adolescence, the age of autonomy. Like infancy, adolescence has its time and place and its own defining freedom. But, if they endure, their times and tasks outlived, each of these first forms of freedom enslaves with iron bands. Whether "Sartrean man"—those company directors in short pants, who take themselves with literally desperate seriousness—is mad or damned we do not need to know. On either diagnosis they require redemption; they need to be set free.

"The necessity of the task [of adulthood] is the choice of finitude, which for us (even after God) means the acknowledgment of the existence of finite others, which is to say, the choice of community, of autonomous moral existence."[11] These are sensible sentiments, but how did that little parenthesis "even after God" get in? The presupposition is clearly similar to that in Horkheimer's claim that "mankind loses religion as it moves through history," but we perhaps need to distinguish between the loss of religion and the disappearance of God.

In its simplest form, the story of "secularization," as told until recently, went something like this. Descartes could take human freedom to be the form of our likeness to God because he, very early modern that he was, had not yet observed the antinomy on which Marx (following Feuerbach) put his finger. But once the "contradictions of theology" were unmasked, it could only be a matter of time before the "true or anthropological essence of religion" was plain to view; and this essence, in turn, its errors and illusions banished and dispelled, might leave at least such traces as Horkheimer's memory of the thirst for perfect justice setting constraints to tyranny.[12]

One difficulty with this story, of course, is that in fact, from the Pentagon to Teheran, from the hills of Peru to the corridors of the Vatican, from India to southern Africa, the world is *awash* with religion. The loss of religion did not, after all, occur. It is as easy, at present, to imagine a militant atheist being elected President of the United States as it is realistic to suppose that the next ruler of Iran will be a Roman Catholic.

This all makes the theologian's task not easier but much more difficult. The practical falsification of at least the more simplistic versions of the secularization thesis has not been accompanied by any significant reconsideration of a key element in its theory. Religion may, for better and for worse, flourish on every side, but God, it seems, is dead. "Getting rid of theology as part of the intellectual life of the West," says Richard Rorty, "was not the achievement of one book nor one man, nor one generation, nor one century."[13] Nevertheless, he has not the slightest doubt that the job has now been done.

One effect of this olympian arrogance is to make all mention of God within its ambience *trivial*. In the mainstream traditions of both Judaism and Christianity, it is a defining feature of serious theological enquiry that finding proper uses for the word *God* is known to be dauntingly difficult, to demand the most extended efforts of our minds and hearts, our logic, integrity, and imagination. It must be so, for to talk lightly of the Holy One is to talk of something else. There is, as it were, a sense of fragility, of risk, of excitement and temerity, in all serious theological speech, and it is just these qualities which disappear when the question of God loses its urgency and interest for believers and nonbelievers alike.

Nietzsche saw this coming: the unconcern of those who had killed God convinced the Madman in *The Gay Science* that they did not understand what their knives had done.[14] The resultant juxtaposition in our culture (which Nietzsche surely did not foresee) of religious exuberance and theological paralysis is both unprecedented and very dangerous. Religion undisciplined by wisdom is as destructive as sexual activity unconstrained by love.

My aims in this paper are much more modest than these large comments might suggest. It is widely supposed, by believers and nonbelievers alike, that faith in God takes the pressure off our finitude, rescues us from "aloneness"; that it sets us free from the constraints of finitude by setting us in relation to a (real or imaginary) reassuring "absolute." Thus, for example, when Kai Nielsen denies that "all reflective atheists are tortured souls despairingly longing for the absolute,"[15] he clearly supposes that it is "the absolute" which is the object of religious faith. Against the grain of this widespread deep assumption, I want to indicate what it might mean to say (adapting Cavell's description of our duty "after God") that the necessity of the task of adulthood is the choice of finitude before God. Adulthood, thus construed, would be a matter of discovering that it is possible, without diminution of dignity, abdication of rationality, or loss of freedom, to yield to what we know and be commanded by it. Such discovery would, nevertheless, be both dark and painful, for its pattern was set in the garden of Gethsemane.

TRANSCENDING AUTONOMY

Nobody familiar with Hegel's *Phenomenology* could sensibly suppose that "absolute" freedom might be a proper goal of ethical and political activity. Freedom, in order to set us free, requires determinants, forms, shapes, configurations. Freedom is not a substance, a force, an entity. The functions of *free* are adjectival: it qualifies our account of actions, arrangements, patterns of relationship, and does not of itself furnish us with materials for their description. Freedom is always particular, finite, contestable, and vulnerable. It is not the name of our home or the description of our destiny but, at best, how we are at home and, at worst, how we may be at sea.

The point is so obvious and elementary that it would not need making were it not for the fact that the characteristically modern notion of freedom as autonomy, a notion first forged in resistance against absolutism, has itself again and again been absolutized and thus proved pregnant with fresh forms of tyranny and inhumanity.

One corrective to this tendency might be the insistence that freedom, for its flourishing, demands articulation with other values such as truth and justice. Then, instead of setting any one single value on an imperial throne, we might get on with the more modest, practical, and demanding business of seeking and struggling for particular, finite configurations and achievements of justice, and truth — and freedom. We have done damage enough with the worship of absolutes. It is surely time to learn the discipline of adulthood, the transcending of autonomy in community and finitude.

Such things are easily said, but where might such discipline be learned? And what would be the manner of its pedagogy? The ethics and the politics of such questions are not my present concern. I confine myself, instead, to some comments on their implications for religion and theology.

Religious maturity, I suggest, is a matter of learning to worship while yet not worshipping oneself or any other thing. Christianity and Judaism, when true to their common structuring convictions, have always been iconoclastic, and their iconoclasm has been rooted in suspicion of idolatry. Idolatry is the divinizing, the taking as absolute and overriding, of any value, fact, nation, dream, project, person, possession, or idea. It matters not what being I take as god and set my heart upon, whether it be freedom or efficiency, yesterday or tomorrow, America or me; to make of some being, of *any* being, an "absolute," an object of worship, is idolatry.

But if the worship of oneself or any other thing is to be contested and deplored, is it not then time, gently and without regret, simply to set an end to worshipping? Once we have learned the lesson that there is no thing, in heaven above or earth below, or in the waters under the earth, which is or could be the proper object of our worship, then what reasons are there left for worshipping? What would the point of worship be?

I do not want to say there is no point to worship, or that we worship for no reason. To do so would suggest that worship is irrational and arbitrary. I do not, as a matter of fact, believe mature and tested human hope to be more arbitrary or irrational than stoicism or despair. Whatever our fundamental stance toward the meaning or unmeaning of the world, we can give reasons for it. And yet, whatever that stance, whatever the response that we enact to the question of the point or "followability" of the world, in the last analysis we neither despair nor hope "*because*. . . ."[16]

In order to render the notion of appropriate worship a little less obscure, consider it in the twofold light of the critique of "foundationalism" and the doctrine of grace. To take the latter angle first: it is a commonplace of Christian doctrine to insist upon the utter, free ungroundedness of God's relation to the world and on that answering ungroundedness or "gratuite," that unconstrained acceptance and response, in which we find our freedom. "Christianity," Karl Rahner once remarked, "would cease to exist if it no longer had the courage to speak of the blessed uselessness of love for God: absolutely useless, since it would not be itself if man were to seek in it his own advantage . . . his own fulfillment."[17]

My reference to appropriate worship was thus intended to paraphrase the notion of love of God "for God's own sake." But both expressions are unsatisfactory, mine because it makes no mention of God, and the classical formula because its anthropomorphism arouses all the familiar suspicions.

After four centuries of modern theism and its antitheses, four centuries of apologetic argument as to why it is that we "need" God to explain the world, it is still too early to know what effect the ending of this episode will have upon the problem of the "naming" of God. It is quite certain, notwithstanding the prejudices of the cultured despisers, that the attempt to make proper mention of God not only will but must continue, because we are always in need of some set of protocols against idolatry. It is idolatry, not faith, which corrupts humanity and frustrates freedom.

Feuerbach, in a most amazing sentence, once announced: "The theory that God cannot be defined, and consequently cannot be known by man, is . . . the offspring of recent times, a product of modern unbelief."[18] The opposite would be nearer the mark. Drawing upon both its Jewish inheritance (in which the impossibility of depicting or naming the Holy One was centrally inscribed) and on Neoplatonism, Christianity — both Eastern and Western — insisted, for more than a millennium and a half, that whatever we say of God is uttered against the silence of a deeper and more fundamental nescience. Whether in the writings of the mystics, or with the grammatical austerity of medieval Scholasticism, the anthropomorphism of our symbols and our narratives was counterpointed and purified by insistence on unknowing.

In the early modern period this dialectic of narrative and nescience, of anthropomorphism and agnosticism, underwent a series of displacements. In the hands of its most influential seventeenth- and eighteenth-century practitioners, Christian theology abandoned its traditional responsibility for the interpretation of Scripture and took for its task and territory the explanation of the natural world. This was a shift not merely of subject matter but of discourse: a shift from formal to material objects or, as we might say, from "grammatical" to "empirical" procedures and concerns. And so, as philosophy developed into "*natural* philosophy," which, in turn, took the form of Newtonian mechanics, the question of God became an empirical affair; and then the hunt was on to prove that somewhere, beyond the particular constituents and movements of the world, a thing, a being, might be found to serve as firm foundation of its existence and explanation of its design.[19] It is, I suggest, the theory that *God* is the name of an object which can not only be defined but located and coordinated with other facts and objects in the world, and known as they are known (namely, by gazing at them); it is this theory which is "the offspring of recent times, the product of modern unbelief." And it is a theory which, in spite of the best efforts of Kant and Hegel (who admirably insisted that "God does not offer himself for observation")[20] is still alive and well in departments of the philosophy of religion.

It is, I think, just possible that the ending of modernity and, with it, the setting to rest of the theisms and a-theisms which were so central to its concerns, may make it *easier* for Christian theology to return to its proper task: the consideration of our identity, our duty and responsibility, in relation to an eternal Word once uttered in a particular time and place.

I apologize for what may have seemed a somewhat lengthy detour from my theme. It was, I think, necessary, in order to indicate the proper background to the suggestion that we do not have nor do we need any idea or image of God except that furnished by the form and flesh of God's appearing. It is not our business, as Christians, to be continually attempting to peer or speculate "beyond" the world in which we live, but rather, *in* that world to find and fashion our human finitude in the form of discipleship. The truth which, according to the Fourth Gospel, shall make us free is truth enfleshed, enacted, made finite and particular, arrested, tried, and crucified, not truth sought elsewhere or somehow found in flight from the circumstances and predicaments and responsibilities and darkness of the world.

ON NOT TAKING FLIGHT

I have spoken of our need to transcend autonomy, to move toward adulthood in learning how to yield, in freedom, to what we know and are commanded by. But, if it is indeed adulthood at which we aim, then the transcendence of autonomy, experienced as dignity or as predicament, is a matter not of the transcendence of finitude but, on the contrary, of finitude's acceptance.

"The longing for unrestricted incorporeal freedom lies deep, if not in human nature, then certainly in the culture to which we belong. The craving to burst out of the bounds of body and of time may well be exactly what it takes to free animals of our kind into the space of culture and history; but it is an ambivalent gift. If we never learn to own our finitude we remain tormented by a powerful inability ever to be satisfied by *anything*."[21] This place, this time, this flesh, these facts, these people: are we in place here? Or are we out of place, in exile, nostalgically restless, "just visiting"? Central to the Jewish and Christian doctrines of creation, and specifically to their refinement in the doctrine of creation *ex nihilo*, is the conviction that this body, this finite fact, is our place and may, in God's graciousness, be made our home.[22]

Lacking the courage, the tranquillity, the self-knowledge, to find our freedom here, we flee. Our flight takes one of two forms.[23] The first is the flight into feeling, on the run from darkness, inhumanity, and impending chaos, in the cultivation of oases of private satisfaction. Whatever we make of William James's claim that drunkenness stands, "to the poor and unlettered . . . in the place of symphony concerts and of literature"[24] (a claim which bites both ways), it would be difficult to deny that the upsurge of "religiousness" in Western culture, of piety peddled as balm for frightened and alienated subjectivity, suggests that narcotic uses of religion are still as widespread and as influential as they were in Marx's day. All forms of the flight into feeling, however, are evasive of finitude, doomed attempts to find our freedom elsewhere than in the particular, public, fleshly facts, relationships, responsibilities, and requirements that determine our existence in the world.

Our other favorite form of flight is the flight into thought, the quest for reassuringly comprehensive explanations of the world. It makes little difference whether or not the explanatory schemes that we devise do or do not include some use or mention of the word *God*, because all such schemes leave the bleakness of the facts around us more or less unchanged. Pushing back the frontiers of knowledge may increase our power but does not necessarily contribute to the transmutation of fate into freedom. And neither metaphysics nor cosmology feeds the hungry or sets the captives free.

To these two forms of flight there correspond, in Christianity, on the one hand the range of pietisms and rebirths which castigate as infidelity all critical scholarship and strenuous engagement of the mind and, on the other, the rationalisms which, impatient of darkness and unknowing, construct remarkably detailed positive descriptions of the nature and attributes of God.

However widespread and influential these two forms of flight have been, they happily do not exhaust the diversity of Christianity. According to Matthew's Gospel, at the moment of Jesus' arrest by the authorities "all the disciples forsook him and fled" (Matt. 26:56). And yet there have always been some brought back to the place and task of Calvary: the reconstruction, in reconciled relationship and the making of community, of what John Milbank calls a "counter-history of peace."[25] This counter-history happens through that occurrence of community which both expresses and makes possible the worship "in Spirit" of the unknown God.[26]

We do not find our freedom in escaping from the flesh, in attempting to set our sights beyond the condition of our finitude, upon some glimpse of an absolute we might call God. As I put it earlier: we do not have nor do we need any idea or image of God except that furnished in the form and flesh of God's appearing.

This is not, of course, an original suggestion of my own. However forgetful of it modern discussions of theism may often have become, it has been, in fact, a central theme in Christian theology at least since the time of the writing of the Fourth Gospel: "Philip said to him, 'Lord, show us the Father, and we shall be satisfied.' Jesus said to him, 'Have I been with you so long, and yet you do not know me, Philip? He who has seen me has seen the Father; how can you say, "Show me the Father"?'" (John 14: 8–9). I would therefore like to close by quoting a remarkable passage from the fourteenth-century English mystic Julian of Norwich. "At this time," she says,

> I wanted to look away from the cross, but I did not dare, for I knew well that whilst I contemplated the cross I was secure and safe. . . . Then there came a suggestion, seemingly said in friendly manner, to my reason: Look up to heaven to his Father. . . . Here I must look up or else answer. I answered inwardly with all the power of my soul, and said: No, I cannot, for you are my heaven. I said this because I did not want to look up. . . . For I knew well that he who had bound me so fast would unbind me when it was his will. So was I taught to choose Jesus for my heaven, whom I saw only in pain at that time. . . . And that has taught me that I should always do so, to choose only Jesus to be my heaven, in well-being and in woe.[27]

Notwithstanding the seemingly friendly manner in which the suggestion was recommended to her reason, the Lady Julian resisted, and would not look beyond the crucified, to heaven to find the Father. Her discipline displays the recognition that, in that figure, freedom is best determined and discerned. The poem of the cross requires to be twice read: first as the form of God's freedom for the world, and then as the form of the human freedom to be found in God. There is, I think, a fascinating affinity between the Lady Julian's restraint and that exhibited in Max Horkheimer's refusal to indulge in "thoughtless optimism." There is also, of course, a difference which is no less profound. For Horkheimer, the concept of infinity was to be preserved in memory as ground and basis for resistance against tyranny. In Lady Julian's reading, the concept also serves to point toward a future: to indicate the unknown substance of our human hope.

NOTES

1. *Dominant ethos* is, actually, too strong, not least because, in the cacophony which currently stands substitute for moral conversation, there is no *one* account which sets the tone.
2. Edward Craig, *The Mind of God and the Works of Man* (Oxford: Clarendon Press, 1987).
3. René Descartes, "Principles of Philosophy" (37), in *The Philosophical Writings of Descartes*, vol. 1, trans. John Cottingham, Robert Stoothoff, Dugald Murdoch (Cambridge: At the University Press, 1985), p. 205. On the significance of the theological overtones to this description, see Craig, *Mind of God*, p. 25.
4. Karl Marx, *Early Writings*, trans. Rodney Livingstone, and Gregory Benton (Harmondsworth: Penguin Books, 1975), pp. 256, 86; see Nicholas Lash, *A Matter of Hope: A Theologian's Reflections on the Thought of Karl Marx* (London: Darton Longman & Todd, 1981), p. 178.
5. William James, *Pragmatism and the Meaning of Truth*, intro. A. J. Ayer, ed. Frederick Burkhardt, Fredson Bowers, and Ignas K. Skrupskelis (Cambridge, Mass.: Harvard University Press, 1978), pp. 221-22.
6. Craig, *Mind of God*, pp. 271, 282.
7. Jean-Paul Sartre, *Being and Nothingness*, trans. Hazel E. Barnes (London: Methuen, 1958), pp. 440-41, cited in Craig, *Mind of God*, p. 304.
8. Max Horkheimer, "Thoughts on Religion," in *Critical Theory*, trans. M. O'Connell et al. (New York: Continuum, 1972), p. 131. McLellan's comment on this passage is: "The legacy of religion was the idea of perfect justice which, while it might be impossible of realisation in this world, yet served as a constant basis of opposition to the powers that were" (David McLellan, *Marxism and Religion* [London: MacMillan, 1987], p. 135).
9. Max Horkheimer, letter to Lowenthal of August, 1946, cited in Martin Jay, *The Dialectical Imagination: A History of the Frankfurt School and the Institute of Social Research 1923-1950* (London: Heinemann, 1973), p. 274.
10. Stanley Cavell, *The Claim of Reason* (Oxford: Clarendon Press, 1979), p. 496.
11. Ibid., p. 464.

12. See, in George Eliot's translation of Feuerbach's *Essence of Christianity*, the chapter headings to the second part and the title of the first.

13. Richard Rorty, *Consequences of Pragmatism* (Minneapolis: University of Minnesota Press, 1982), p. 34.

14. See Michael J. Buckley, *At the Origins of Modern Atheism* (New Haven, Conn.: Yale University Press, 1987), pp. 28–30. Not the least of the good reasons for resisting Rorty's claim that theology has been disposed of is that, as Buckley insists, it remains important to ask *what* god died beneath those knives.

It is a pity that Rorty would be unlikely to have the patience to work through the section on "Bonhoeffer's Contribution to the Return of 'Death of God' Talk to Theology," in Eberhard Jungel, *God as the Mystery of the World: On the Foundation of the Theology of the Crucified One in the Dispute between Theism and Atheism*, trans. Darrell L. Guder (Edinburgh, T. & T. Clark, 1983), pp. 57–63.

For drawing my attention to this passage, and for suggesting a number of similarities between the drift of my argument and the main thrust of Bonhoeffer's mature theology, I am grateful to Gareth Jones.

15. Kai Nielsen, "God and Coherence: On the Epistemological Foundations of Religious Belief," in *Knowing Religiously*, ed. Leroy S. Rouner (Notre Dame, Ind.: University of Notre Dame Press, 1985), p. 101.

16. On the relationship between faith and "followability" (a concept borrowed by Frank Kermode from W. B. Gallie), see Nicholas Lash, "How Do We Know Where We Are?" in *Theology on the Way to Emmaus* (London: SCM Press, 1986), pp. 62–74.

17. Karl Rahner, "The Inexhaustible Transcendence of God and Our Concern for the Future," in *Theological Investigations*, vol. 20, trans. Edward Quinn (London: Darton Longman & Todd, 1981), p. 180.

18. Ludwig Feuerbach, *The Essence of Christianity*, trans. George Eliot, intro. Karl Barth, foreword by H. Richard Niebuhr (New York: Harper & Row, 1957), p. 14.

19. This story and its consequences have recently been magisterially expounded by Michael J. Buckley, *At the Origins of Modern Atheism* (New Haven and London: Yale University Press, 1987), on which see Nicholas Lash, "When Did the Theologians Lose Interest in Theology?" in *Theology and Dialogue*, ed. Bruce D. Marshall (forthcoming).

See also Nicholas Lash, "Observation, Revelation, and the Posterity of Noah," in *Physics, Philosophy, and Theology: A Common Quest for Understanding*, ed. Robert John Russell, William R. Stoeger, and George V. Coyne (Notre Dame, Ind.: University of Notre Dame Press, 1988), pp. 203–15.

20. G. W. F. Hegel, *Lectures on the Philosophy of Religion*, vol. 1: *Introduction and the Concept of Religion*, ed. Peter C. Hodgson (Berkeley: University of California Press, 1984), p. 313.

21. Fergus Kerr, *Theology after Wittgenstein* (Oxford: Basil Blackwell, 1986), p. 45.

22. See Edward Schillebeeckx's analysis of the doctrine of creation in *God among Us: The Gospel Proclaimed* (London: SCM Press, 1983), discussed by Kerr, *Theology after Wittgenstein*, pp. 184–85; see also Richard J. Clifford, "The Hebrew Scriptures and the Theology of Creation," *Theological Studies* 46 (1985): 507–23.

23. See Nicholas Lash, *Easter in Ordinary: Reflections on Human Experience and the Knowledge of God* (Charlottesville: University Press of Virginia, 1988), pp. 280–85.

24. William James, *The Varieties of Religious Experience*, intro. John E. Smith, in *The Works of William James*, ed. Frederick H. Burkhardt, Fredson Bowers, and Ignas K. Skrupskelis (Cambridge, Mass.: Harvard University Press, 1985), p. 307.

25. John Milbank, "The Second Difference: For a Trinitarianism without Reserve," *Modern Theology* 2 (1986): 227.

26. For an account of the character and possibility of such community slightly less bleak than that offered by Alasdair MacIntyre in *After Virtue*, see Nicholas Lash, "The Church's Responsibility for the Future of Humanity," in *Theology on the Way to Emmaus*, pp. 186–201.

27. Julian of Norwich, *Showings*, trans. and intro. Edmund Colledge and James Walsh (New York: Paulist Press, 1978), pp. 211–21.

2
Is Protestantism the "Religion of Freedom"?
JÜRGEN MOLTMANN

> It is no longer worthwhile to pursue the fate of German Protestantism. Four hundred years of a glorious history are coming to an end. What will still remain of a folk religion in Europe in a hundred years will be Catholic.[1]

SO WROTE THE WELL-KNOWN German journalist Johannes Gross in the *Frankfurter Allgemeine Zeitung* in 1987.

Is this sad prediction true, or is it just Catholic wishful thinking? What was Protestantism? What is Protestantism? Does Protestantism have a future? Which form will Protestantism take in the transition from modernity to a postmodern age?

Do we still long for religious freedom and the freedom of religion, or are we afraid of the risks of freedom and tired of having to make too many choices alone? Do we really want "Freedom now!" or are we finally weary of the responsibility inseparably bound up with freedom? Do we really want to grow up, or are we longing for a child's religious tutelage from "Mother Church" or "Father State" or "Daddy Guru"? It may well be that the future of Protestantism and the future of freedom are one and the same destiny.

The Protestant concept of freedom has gone through three formative epochs: (1) the Reformation of the sixteenth century, (2) the Protestantism of the eighteenth-century Enlightenment, and (3) the ecumenism of the twentieth century. In the Reformation the issue was the "religion of the faith"; in the Enlightenment the issue was the "religion of freedom." Today the issue is the ecumenical "religion of the community."

I. "JUSTIFIED BY FAITH ALONE"

The way for the Reformation was prepared by reform movements in the late Middle Ages. The Reformation itself had an immediate effect on several centers of northern Europe about the same time, especially in Wittenberg, Zurich, Geneva, and Strasbourg. From 1521 until 1525 it was a people's movement which spread like wildfire through almost all of Christendom. Nonetheless, for its igniting idea it thanks one man: Martin Luther. His personal confession before Emperor Charles V at the Diet of Worms in 1521, his Reformation pamphlets such as "On the Freedom of a Christian," his magnificent Bible translation, which stamps the German language of poets, thinkers, and the common people even to this day, his catechisms and his hymns, such as "A Mighty Fortress Is Our God," have awakened the Protestant faith and shape it to this day.

The leading idea in this movement is easy to recognize and, as with all great movements, it is simple. It is the recognition of the justifying gospel. "We are justified before God by grace for Christ's sake by faith alone," as the Augsburg Confession of 1530, Article 4, puts it. The righteous God does not judge according to one's merits or bad works; rather God accepts sinful humans out of pure love and for Christ's sake makes them righteous and good. That was Luther's "Reformation recognition": God is righteous because God makes righteous. The righteousness of God is not a righteousness that establishes facts (*justitia distributiva*) but rather a creative righteousness (*justitia justificans*). It is revealed in Christ "who was put to death for our trespasses and raised for our justification" (Rom. 4:25).

That is why justifying faith alone is the true knowledge of Christ, and the true knowledge of Christ leads to justifying faith. The doctrine of justification is indeed the center and limit of Reformation theology. Luther called it the "articulus stantis et candentis ecclesiae." That is why he did not want to give in to his opponents on this doctrine: "May Heaven and Earth then fall or whatever else does not want to stay there."[2] The clarity of the doctrine of justification decides whether the church is the church of God's gospel or a Christian religious institution. It decides whether a real human being believes in the true God or chases after her or his own idols. The object of Christian theology is then according to Luther "the justifying God and the sinful human."[3] God's salvific acting through Christ for confused and lost humans is the essential content of Christian theology. Reformation faith is again, as in the New Testament period, faith in Christ, the Christ who was crucified for us. Christ is the ground and the criterion of true faith, the true church, and true theology.

The consequences of Reformation faith were far reaching, centering on the four principles of Protestant theology:

A. *Sola fide*

Whoever assents to the God who loves sinners, and by grace justifies them, believes. He or she does not decide for God. He or she recognizes that God has decided for him or her and joyfully says to that, "Yes and Amen." Faith means to make God's verdict one's own, to trust God's promise, to assent to God's justifying grace, even against one's own accusing conscience. If my righteousness were not dependent on God's grace alone but also on my conduct as well, there would be no way I could be certain of my salvation, because then I would never know whether I had also done enough. Only when a person's righteousness is entirely and alone dependent on God's grace is one unambiguously certain of one's salvation, as Paul wrote: "For I am sure that neither death, nor life . . . will be able to separate us from the love of God in Christ our Lord" (Rom. 8:38–39). This personal certainty of one's salvation in life and in death was the central affirmation of the Protestant Reformation.

B. *Sola gratia*

Whoever has become righteous by faith alone can live free of fear. She or he does not need to worry anymore about the salvation of her or his soul. Every worry that she or he has directs itself toward the neighbor. Faith alone makes one blessed.

But faith is never alone; rather it is active in love as long as the person who believes lives. Whoever is righteous by faith alone has become a child of God. Through dependence on good works and merits one never becomes a child of God; rather one always remains a slave. One becomes a child by birth, and a child of God by rebirth out of the Spirit of God. This nobility of the divine birth is the seal of the children of God. The glory of achievement and the verdict according to good works are the seals of the slave. God justifies the sinner and accepts the human person. Whoever believes this experiences a new being in oneself and becomes another person. All our works, the good ones and the evil ones, come out of our being. The good tree brings forth good fruit; the evil tree brings forth evil fruit. The principle "sola gratia" in Protestantism was never the principle of laziness. It has always been the source of restless labor. Whoever is freed from the law of good works overflows with love and does all good works "sua sponte," of one's own accord, out of pure thankfulness. For whoever God has justified by grace hungers for justice in the world and protests against injustice. All those to whom God has given peace in their souls thirst for peace on earth and protest against the discord of the world.

C. *Solus Christus*

The Christian church can then speak with certainty when Christ, and Christ alone, is its Lord. The Christian church comes then in its freedom when it heeds the gospel of Christ alone. That is why all Reformation confessions of faith demand that the statutes, rituals, and symbols of the ecclesiastical tradition and popular belief must be subjected to the standard of Christ. When in Hitler's dictatorship the Protestant church in Germany was supposed to be made fascist, the Confessing Church declared at Barmen in 1934:

> Jesus Christ is the one Word of God that we have to hear. We reject the false teaching, as if the church could or would have to acknowledge as a source of its proclamation besides and next to this Word of God still other events, powers, figures, and truths as God's revelation. . . . We reject the false teaching, as if there were areas of our lives in which we did not belong to Jesus Christ but to other lords.[4]

The Reformation applied this Christocentrism critically to the church of that time. The Confessing Church applied it critically to a dictatorship's claim to control everything, and to its attempt to politicize religion. This exclusive belief in Christ denotes the center of Protestant faith. But because Christ is believed in and confessed as the Lord of the whole world, this is the center for a horizon which reaches as far as the clouds go and embraces all of creation. A correctly understood Christocentrism does not lead astray to narrow-mindedness; rather it leads to true openness to the world.

D. *Sola scriptura*

Scripture alone. That doctrine was directed against the Catholic synthesis: Scripture and tradition, Scripture and a current sense of the faith. Scripture itself is the sufficient witness of the gospel of Jesus Christ that justifies sinners and is comprehensible for everyone who can read. But is Scripture infallible? Is Scripture "the Protestant Pope"? Behind that question is a real theological problem, the problem of the teaching office in the church. The Catholic view is that the teaching authority of the apostles has passed on from Peter to the Bishop of Rome or to the community of bishops. That is why the bishops now speak with apostolic authority in the name of Christ. The Protestant view is that the authority of the apostles has not been transferred to anyone. The apostles were eyewitnesses of the resurrected Christ and for their part did not install any new apostles who were supposed to become their successors. Rather their apostolic authority has passed on to their apostolic writings. Today they speak through the writings of the New Testament and through the church. The first view speaks of a *successio apostolica;* the second view speaks of a *successio evangelica.* Of what use is the formal apostolic succession from one bishop to another when these bishops do not stand in the faithful succession of the proclamation of the gospel according to Scripture?

Out of these four Protestant principles follows a new understanding of the church and of being a Christian in the world. Because God also calls every Christian who has been justified by means of the gospel, in the church of Christ the *general priesthood of all believers* prevails. "Whoever has crawled out of baptism is ordained priest and pope," wrote Martin Luther in 1520.[5] I add to that: men *and women*. With that Luther wanted to tear down the wall that separates clergy and laypeople in the church. All called Christians belong to the One People of God which represents altogether "an elected race and a royal priesthood." By tracing the ordination as priest (*sacramentum ordinis*) back to baptism, Luther raised the value of baptism so that it became the sacrament of the call. Every Christian is a witness of the faith, called to proclamation of the gospel and to celebration of the Lord's Supper. Where this recognition was taken seriously, the congregation, the concrete gathering of the faithful, took the place of the hierarchy of priests.

Whomever God justifies, God calls as well. That is the case not only in the church of Christ but also in everyday life. With great genius Luther transferred the concept of the "call" (*vocatio*) from the religious sphere to the secular sphere and called every form of labor that one does one's "calling." With this move he introduced the principles of the divine call, such as obedience, faithfulness, love, reliability, and collaboration with the Kingdom of God, into secular labor. Every honest vocation is a "service to God." Every form of labor or employment in society is Kingdom-of-God-employment and derives its higher meaning from this orientation. The Protestant work ethic developed out of this view. In Lutheranism it was the world of established social stations that was perceived as the divine order. In Calvinism it was the world of the small and large entrepreneurs who worked, saved, and invested for the Kingdom of God.

But both these points also indicate the weakness of the Reformation. It remained in the sixteenth century an "incomplete Reformation."

In the Formation of the Church

Because the congregational church (*Gemeindekirche*) could not be realized, the freedom of the church from the power of the state could not be established independently. Formerly that freedom had been guaranteed by the pope. Now came the Protestant "prince church," a territorial church under the authority of the prince. The territorial ruler was enlisted as an "emergency bishop." The ruler organized the Protestant church as a territorial church according to the principle: "Cujus regio, ejus religio." The Protestant church had to give up its universality, and it turned into particularistic national churches. It fell into a new Constantinian captivity from which it has been freed only by the ecumenical movement of our century.

In the Formation of Being a Christian

If the society in which Christians exist is a "Christian world," then one could identify the spiritual call of a Christian with his or her social or political vocation. But in a post-Christian world this is no longer possible. The spiritual call of every Christian is something special and must show itself in the "special righteousness" of the Christian in this secular world. This "special righteousness" appears when Christians in the midst of the contradictions of the secular society enter upon the discipleship of Christ according to the directives of the Sermon on the Mount. They then demonstrate to this violent and unjust society the divine alternative which leads to peace and to life.

Nevertheless, the message of the Reformation was experienced by many people as incomparably liberating. It was the experience of freedom in faith. According to Luther's 1520 pamphlet, "On the Freedom of a Christian," freedom was opened by the justifying Word of God to all who believe. Faith makes them "free masters of all things." They are no one's subjects. Love makes them "useful servants of all things." They are everyone's subjects.[6]

From what does the Word of Christ free those who believe? According to Reformation theology, it frees them from compulsion to sin, from the law of self-justification, and from fear of death. Sin, the law, and death are the three great godless powers of the world.

To what does the Word of Christ free those who believe? It frees them to unimpeded, direct, and eternal communion with God. In faith all have access to the Father. In faith all become children of God. In faith we all become friends of God whose prayer God hears. In faith we are in God and God is in us.

Freedom in faith is a relational and theological concept of freedom. In relation to humans, the justifying God becomes the liberating God. In their relationship to God, justified humans become free humans. In God's covenant with humankind freedom is defined from God's perspective as righteousness and from the perspective of humankind as faith.

II. THE RELIGION OF FREEDOM

The Protestant faith entered into a particularly close alliance with the new culture of the Enlightenment, humanism, and religious tolerance in the seventeenth and eighteenth centuries. The bourgeois world of the nineteenth century was for many "the Protestant world," especially in Great Britain, Prussia-Germany, and the United States. The idea of Protestantism is revealed in this modern form of the Protestant faith.

But what is Enlightenment? I am using two definitions of Immanuel Kant, the "philosopher of Protestantism": (1) "Enlightenment is man's exit from his state of not being of age, which he brought about by his own fault";[7] and (2) "For this Enlightenment is nothing more required than the freedom to make public use of his reason in all parts."[8]

We need to distinguish between the English-American Enlightenment and the Enlightenment in France and Germany. The English-American Enlightenment was Protestant-dominated, nonconformist, free church, and very religious, as one can still see in the United States every Sunday. The French Enlightenment, on the other hand, was anticlerical and dominated by opposition to any and all ecclesiastical influence. Its humanism was areligious and atheistic through and through. The German Enlightenment was shaped by Protestantism but directed against the state churches. It championed the right of the individual to personal religion and shared the utopian dream of the "coming Kingdom of the Spirit" in which no one would have to teach anyone else anything because in the Spirit all see God as God is.

The Christianity of the Enlightenment can be found in the new Protestant denominations of that time: the Quakers with the religious experience of the "inner light of the Spirit," the Baptists with the personal decision of faith, and the Methodists with their heartwarming experience of faith and personal sanctification through self-control and self-command. "Soul Liberty" was the new catchword (Roger Williams). The discovery of the individual and of the right to subjectivity dominates modern Protestantism.

In Germany the Christian confession has been an affair of state since the Peace of Westphalia in 1648, which ended the Thirty Years' War ("cujus regio, ejus religio"). Religious freedom existed only as *jus emigrandi*. That is why Christianity in bourgeois Protestantism became privatized with such slogans as "Religion is a private affair," and "Everyone should make themselves happy in their own way." Protestantism in England and in the United States created ideas of voluntary religion. Here religious freedom means that every person has the right to worship and revere God in the church of her or his choice. In Germany this was not the case. The discrepancy remained between religious identity and voluntary religious activity, between state religion and private faith, between institutionalism and subjectivism. As always in Germany, there was no freedom to make public use of one's personal faith in all respects. Even today 90 percent of the German people belong to a church, but only 10 to 15 percent go to their church. In Germany religious freedom was without exception perceived only as the right to "internal emigration" from the institutional church.

The principles of the Enlightenment and of Protestantism are the principles of the freedom of the individual:

A. *Freedom of Religion over against the State*

As long as the state determines the religion or ideology, individuals remain minors without control over their own behavior. They can exercise neither their reason nor their faith without the guidance of another person. Freedom of religion for every individual is therefore a presupposition of Protestant faith as well as a presupposition of reason. Freedom of religion frees religion from the state and the state from religion. It is then reasonable for the state to be tolerant of religion. After freedom of religion had been achieved in England in the seventeenth century it was introduced in France in 1789, and with corresponding delays it hesitantly spread in Germany. And in Vatican II it was finally acknowledged by the Roman Catholic Church.

B. Freedom of Conscience over against the Church

As long as the church binds the conscience of individuals in ethical questions, the individuals are not in control of their own behavior. They are minors, dependents. That is why the Enlightenment freed the conscience first of all. In one's conscience every single person stands directly before God and must decide for oneself. Conscience was called "the God within us" (Kant) to safeguard its inviolability. For many, Protestantism became the "religion of conscience" (K. Holl). The church can sharpen the conscience of individuals; but it is not allowed to take the decision of conscience away from anyone—either by encyclical or pastoral letters—because what the individual does or does not do the church cannot or does not have to answer for before God. The church is also not allowed to seduce anyone to act against their conscience. This has been the Christian view from time immemorial.

C. Freedom of Belief over against Religious Authorities

In spite of the authority of the Bible, the tradition, and the church, I have the right to my own conviction and to my own doubts. As Lessing, the reformer of the German Enlightenment, said, "Some things are miracles which I see with my own eyes and have the opportunity to test. Others are miracles which I only know from history that other persons claim to have seen and tested" (*Werke* 3.9). One is a chance truth of history mediated in good faith, another a necessary truth of reason immediately comprehensible to me. "It is one thing to believe the truth out of prejudice, another thing to believe it for its own sake" (*Werke* 3.127). It is one thing to do good out of fear of punishment, another thing to do good because it is good.

D. Freedom of Conscience and the Individual's Freedom of Belief

Over against the church, as divine institution "from above," these individual freedoms establish the right to community gathered "from below." The church is simply the community assembled at a certain place and time. Community was the original promise of the Reformation, but that promise was hindered by the

Protestant system of church government which set up the local ruler as the head of his or her territorial church.

The rights of freedom of religion, freedom of faith, freedom of conscience, and freedom of community were achieved in the age of the Enlightenment together with other human rights and civil rights. By means of these rights the dignity of the human person is publicly acknowledged. Even today freedom of religion cannot be realized apart from the rights of freedom of the person and individual human rights. The bourgeoisie achieved these rights of freedom in the English, American, and French Revolutions against feudalism and clericalism. The rights of freedom of religion, freedom of faith, and freedom of conscience became the foundation of liberal democracy.

E. The Personal Dimensions of Freedom

Modern Protestantism changes the Reformation's *freedom in faith* into the *freedom of faith*, that is, freedom for the personal decision of faith. The subjective concept of freedom of choice was added to the relational concept of freedom before the justifying God. The subjectivity of every single human person now came into its own and stamped the human side of the communion with God. Pressing on to a personal decision of faith, a personal conversion experience, and the heartwarming, internal witness of the Holy Spirit could lead to a new Pelagianism and a new works righteousness in modern Protestant denominations; but it does not have to, as one can see with John Wesley, who reached back to Luther himself. Yet Reformation Christocentrism has experienced a pneumatological addition and sharpening. Freedom, by means of the Word of God, is also freedom in the Spirit of God. No state and no church can take away from individuals the personal decision of faith or rob them of their personal experiences of the divine Spirit.

"Subjectivity is truth," said the Protestant thinker Kierkegaard. Protestant subjectivism, religious and cultural, has certainly led to all possible forms of individualism, pluralism, and egoism. But it has also brought the dignity of every human person and individual human rights unforgettably into modern culture. Without freedom of belief and personal responsibility, a humane society is not possible. All postmodern attempts to overcome human subjectivity simply abolish humanity, be it by means of the bureaucratic conspiracy or the Aquarian Conspiracy.

III. THE RELIGION OF THE COMMUNITY

The Protestant churches have been moving out of the confessional age into the ecumenical age for roughly eighty years, and they were the first to do so. In the process they have discovered more and more the meaning of catholicity in the Church of Christ, and they seek in the ecumenical movement of the separate churches the community of the Holy Spirit. For many Protestant Christians today the ecumenical solidarity with oppressed brothers and sisters in other lands and other confessions is more important than national loyalty or their own confessional identity. Ecumenical community is the discovery of the other and the reciprocal acceptance of the other in his or her differentness.

A. *Living Ecumenically*

The way to ecumenical understanding between the separate churches began with work on comparative ecclesiology. One got to know one another in the hope that "a better understanding of the diverging opinions on faith and church order will lead to a deepening of the wish for reunification and to corresponding official decisions of the confessions," as it was said at the Missionary Conference in Edinburgh in 1910.[9] The result is a sort of negative consensus. One discovers that the traditional distinguishing teachings do not necessarily have to separate the churches. They can also be used reciprocally to supplement and enrich one's own teachings. One found therefore in the different theological and ecclesiological traditions no reason anymore for a separation that excommunicates but still could not formulate something in common that binds. Not until the General Assembly of the World Council of Churches at Lund in 1952 did christological ecclesiology replace comparative ecclesiology: "We have recognized that we cannot make any real progress toward unity when we only compare with one another our different conceptions of the essence of the church and the different traditions in which they are embedded. It appeared that we come closer to one another in that we come closer to Christ. Therefore we must pierce all the way through our schisms to a deeper and richer understanding of the mystery of the unity of God with his church, which God has given us in Christ."[10] This turn from the merely external comparative ecclesiology to the internally binding christological ecclesiology has determined the ecumenical movement since that time. The closer we come to Christ, the closer we come to one another.

Ecumenical community arises everywhere in the world where we find ourselves under Christ's cross as brothers and sisters, as hungry people in common poverty (Rom. 3:23), as prisoners in common sin. Under his cross we are all standing there with empty hands. We have nothing to offer except the burden of guilt and the emptiness of our hearts. Under the cross of Christ Protestants, Catholics, and Orthodox are not counted. There the godless are justified, enemies reconciled, prisoners freed, the poor made rich, and the sad filled with hope. That is why we also discover ourselves under the cross of Christ as children of Christ's freedom and as friends in the community of the Spirit. "The closer we come to the cross of Christ, the closer we come to one another." How can we maintain our schisms and animosities in the face of his bitter suffering and death? How can we remain closed in the face of the "open heart of Christ" and fear for the Church? How can we — moved by the arms of God stretched out in suffering on the cross — ball our fists or with cramped hands hold tight to our confessional property?

B. Thinking Ecumenically

When Christians and entire churches leave the narrow horizons of their particular traditions and confessions and recognize the sweeping ecumenical horizon, rethinking begins. This learning process, which one can observe in oneself, is bound up with the pains and joys of conversion. One begins to overcome particularistic thinking. Particularistic thinking is an isolating, fragmentary, and self-satisfying way of thinking, a way of thinking that, because it only knows and wants to confirm itself, appears with the claim of absoluteness. We cannot endure our own particularity, limitedness, and relativity. That is why individuals and entire groups obstinately cling to their possessions. They are possessed by fear and sow fear all around them. Particularistic thinking is fundamentally schismatic thinking. In the age of church schisms and confessional absolutism we have grown so accustomed to schismatic thinking that some do not notice it anymore. We define our limits by comparing ourselves to others. We assert ourselves and our heritage. That is what one not long ago called "controversial theology." It was theology in the service of church schisms and confessional self-assertion. To think ecumenically means to overcome schismatic thinking. That is only possible when particularistic thinking is overcome by a universal way of thinking. How does that come about?

One can consider the witnesses of faith and life in Christendom from the perspective of particularity. Then there are Orthodox, Catholic, Protestant, and still other witnesses, and understanding ends with the recognition: that is Orthodox; that is Catholic; that Anglican; and that Lutheran.

But one can also consider these witnesses from the perspective of their universality. Then one understands them as utterances of the one and whole Church. Then one tests them in this universal horizon and responds in this community. Theological thinking does not thereby become easier; rather it becomes harder because one can then no longer blame the problems and controversies on the difference in confession. Ecumenical thinking means: Consider the whole, the whole of the one Church.

If schismatic thinking consists of regarding one's own part as the whole and making it absolute, then ecumenical thinking dissolves this syndrome of fear and arrogance and makes it possible consciously to exist incompletely, limited, open for others and dependent upon others. The claim of truth upon us — not our claim upon truth — is absolute. The divine kingdom — not our ecclesiastical domains — is all-encompassing. I believe it is a strength of ecumenical thinking to awaken desire for the other through recognition of one's own incompleteness. Therefore, ecumenical thinking also means: Consider that you are only one part of the one Church.

C. *The Social Dimensions of Freedom*

In the age of the ecumenical community Protestants discover the social dimensions of justification and the communicative concept of freedom. They discover what the catholicity of Christendom means. They understand solidarity with the suffering and the oppressed. They learn to understand that true freedom does not mean dominion, but community. Human freedom does not consist in the formal concept of the power of disposition of property. Nor does human freedom lie in freedom of choice, according to which I can do what I want to. These formal concepts of freedom originate from the language of dominion. Modern individualism has not changed anything in that regard when it maintains that every human is his or her own "sovereign" and belongs to him- or herself. The specific human concept of freedom, on the other hand, originates from the language of community. Here *freedom* means the same thing as *friendship:* I feel completely free where I can be completely myself. I can only be completely myself where I am known and appreciated and accepted as I am. I become free where I open my life for others and appreciate them in their differentness and am gladly together with them. Human freedom is realized by means of mutual appreciation and acceptance, that is, in personal communion. Then the other person is no longer a limit to my freedom. The other enlarges my limited life.

This is the social and the communicative side of human freedom. We call it solidarity or friendship or love. By means of this solidarity, the Reformation ideal of justification by faith and the Protestant ideal of freedom of belief are fully realized: "Accept one another, therefore, as Christ has accepted you, for the glory of God" (Rom. 15:7). We seek and experience the reality of freedom in narrower and broader horizons: in the ecumenical community of different Christians, in the community of solidarity with the oppressed, and in communion with the threatened creation.

SUMMARY

A. Protestant faith is faith in the justifying gospel of Christ. This faith brings personal certainty of salvation. In this faith men and women are called to all forms of service in the Church of Christ and to all forms of service in the world—everyone according to one's abilities, and everyone according to one's needs.

B. The idea of Protestantism is the modern, bourgeois, human form of the Protestant faith. Subjectivity stands in the foreground: the personal decision of faith, the individual decision of conscience, freedom and responsibility for one's life.

C. The ecumenical form of Protestant faith lies in the discovery of the transnational and transconfessional catholicity of the Church of Christ. This recognition was won in times of persecution, that is, "under the cross." It leads one to press forward to the eucharistic communion at the table of the Lord. Living ecumenically means to hunger and thirst for the eucharistic communion of all Christians. Thinking and acting ecumenically means to hunger and thirst for God's righteousness for the whole world. Both the ecumenical community inside the church and the Christian ecumenical community reaching outward belong together today. In order to enter into the age of humanity's world history, the Church must achieve full ecumenical community.

NOTES

1. *Frankfurter Allgemeine Zeitung*, 2 June 1987.
2. Martin Luther, "Schmalkaldische Artikel" (1537), in *Die Bekenntnisschriften der Evangelisch-Lutherischen Kirche* (Göttingen, 1952), pp. 415f.
3. Luther WA 40.2.
4. A. Burgsmuller and R. Weth, eds., *Die Barmer Theologische Erklärung* (Neukirk, 1983), p. 34. See also B. Klappert, "Barmen I und die Juden," in *Bekennende Kirche wagen: Barmen 1934-1984*, ed. Jürgen Moltmann (Munich, 1984), pp. 59ff.
5. Martin Luther, "De Captivitate Babylonica" (1520), in *Luthers Werke in Auswahl*, ed. Otto Clemen (Berlin, 1929), 1:458ff.
6. Martin Luther, "Von der Freiheit eines Christenmenschen" (1520), in *Luthers Werke in Auswahl*, ed. Clemen, 2:11.
7. Immanuel Kant, *Was ist Aufklärung?* (1784) in *Was ist Aufklärung? Aufsätze zur Geschichte und Philosophie*, ed. J. Zehbe (Göttingen, 1967), p. 55.
8. Ibid., p. 56.
9. Cited in E. Lange, *Die ökumenische Utopie, oder: Was bewegt die ökumenische Bewegung?* (Stuttgart, 1972), p. 37.
10. Ibid., p. 45. See also Jürgen Moltmann, *The Church in the Power of the Spirit*, trans. Margaret Kohl (New York, 1977), pp. 11ff.

3
Freedom, the Self, and the Other
DAVID W. TRACY

I. INTRODUCTION: A QUESTION OF MEANING

IN THE CHRISTIAN THEOLOGICAL tradition, the question of freedom has been a central issue. On the one hand, the Christian interpretation of reality demands an agent who possesses authentic freedom. Since the time of Paul, Christian thought has affirmed the true freedom of the Christian — summarily the gift of freedom in Christ that both empowers and commands the agent to act responsibly before God and for others. Since the time of Augustine, this originally Pauline insight has been at the center of Christian self-interpretation. One aspect of that Augustinian heritage has been developed by the Thomist tradition in Catholic theology ordinarily under the rubric of grace and freedom. The famous, if not notorious, debates on the relationships of grace and freedom in Thomas Aquinas were articulated throughout the centuries since Aquinas' own reflection: the Banezian-Molinist dispute was merely the most famous of the series of impasses of those hermeneutical debates. In our own century, the creative interpretations of Maurice de la Taille (on "actuation"), Karl Rahner (on "quasi-formal causality"), and Bernard Lonergan (on "contingent predication") are probably the most fruitful contemporary interpretations of Thomas Aquinas on this still controverted issue.

The other side of the Augustinian heritage on grace and freedom has been most developed in the Reformation. The classic loci here remain Luther's debate with Erasmus, especially Luther's influential works *The Bondage of the Will* and *The Freedom of the Christian*, as well as Calvin's reflections on predestination. Those debates, too, continue in our day—from the Arminian debates among Calvinists, to the revisionary understandings of the hidden and revealed God of Calvin and Luther in Karl Barth and Brian Gerrish, to the insistence on the primacy of freedom for the Christian understanding of the self in such different theologians as John Cobb, Schubert Ogden, and Robert Neville.

Moreover, the deprivatizing of both Catholic and Protestant theologies by the political, liberation, and feminist theologians has also contributed importantly to new Christian theological reflections on freedom. The insistence on political, economic, and cultural freedom in these theologies has considerably revised any residual purely "private" or individualistic understandings of the self and its freedom. This complex and still developing Christian conflict over freedom can find no easy rehearsal nor resolution in a single essay. For present purposes, it is, perhaps, sufficient to recall some of that history and to suggest a way to formulate the question. There have been fierce controversies both within and between Catholic and Protestant theologies and between more individual-personal understandings of freedom (like Bultmann and Rahner) and more political understandings (like Sölle, Moltmann, Metz, Ruether, and Gutierrez). But they all share this conviction: the self of the Christian receives as gift and command the call to freedom. The Christian is a responsible agent.

I leave aside the question of philosophical, psychological, and sociological interpretations of freedom in order to attempt the following hermeneutical-rhetorical thought experiment. Can one affirm a basic, even communal, Christian scriptural understanding of the self as free agent before God and then see what light that rhetoric of the self may cast on one great alternative contemporary reading? If the principal issue is freedom and determinism, one candidate for such a Christian rhetorical reading is clearly psychoanalytical theory. But the debates within psychoanalytical theory on these issues of freedom are at least as complicated and conflicted as those within Christian theology, so a more limited focus must be found. The recent debate on Jacques Lacan's reading of Freud suggests itself as an admirable candidate for such a reading. I choose this particular debate rather than revisionist Freudianism, especially American ego-psychology, for two reasons: First, I have become persuaded, for reasons that cannot be argued here, that Lacan's reading of Freud is more accurate to Freud's texts than the more familiar revisionist ego-psychology. Second, the notion of the relatively autonomous "ego" of much revisionist Freudianism strikes me as far less fruitful for a Christian theological construal of the self and its freedom than either Freud or Lacan allows.

These two presuppositions of the inquiry, although controversial, need not interfere with the present thought experiment. For even if I am wrong in my appraisals of the relative strength of Lacan's reading of Freud and the relative weakness of American ego-psychology, the Christian theological construals of Freud and Lacan need not be affected. For the present inquiry is not an attempt to correlate the meaning and truth of the Christian view of the self and its freedom in the presence of God with the meaning and truth of the Freud-Lacan psychoanalytic view of the self and its freedom in the presence of the unconscious. Rather, the inquiry is whether a Christian theological rhetorical reading of the self and freedom can illuminate the issues at stake in Lacan's reading of Freud. To resolve this issue, two steps are needed: first, an interpretation of the basic Christian understanding of the self-as-agent and its freedom; second, a use of that interpretation to see what light it may cast on Lacan's reading of Freud.

II. THE CHRISTIAN AGENT: THE NARRATIVE AND ITS PROPHETIC AND MYSTICAL READINGS

There remains, in Christian discourse, a need to see what is common even in order to clarify the nature of the differences. I have elsewhere argued that the main Christian confession remains, "We believe in Jesus the Christ with the apostles." To state the confession as a common confession is, I continue to believe, helpful. For, thus stated, the confession clarifies what Christians both are and are not claiming. What they are claiming may be interpreted as follows. Christians understand the self and its freedom, as well as history and nature, primarily by their affirmation of Jesus Christ as the decisive manifestation of both who God is and who human beings are empowered and commanded to become. By believing *in* this singular Jesus of Nazareth as the Christ, Christians construe all reality anew in that light: who God is, how nature and history are ultimately to be understood, and who the self is in its gifted freedom. To eliminate any element of this central confession is to change the Christian understanding of all reality. For example, the confession is not "We believe in Christ," so that the Sophia-Logos tradition unrelated to the ministry, teaching, death, and resurrection of this Jesus of Nazareth confessed to be the Christ can suffice. Alternatively, the confession is also not "We believe in Jesus," so that some portrait of Jesus can replace the ecclesial Christian confession "We believe in Jesus Christ."

Moreover, the preposition *with* in the phrase "with the apostles" cannot be allowed to be subtly replaced, in effect, by the preposition *in* — so that, in effect, the tradition or doctrine or church or apostolic office or text replaces Jesus Christ as that which the Christian ultimately believes *in*. At the same time, the contemporary Christian believes *in* Jesus Christ *with* the apostles. Aside from the intense inner-Christian debates on what this crucial phrase "with the apostles" means exactly, this much is shared by Christians: the New Testament texts of the early apostolic communities' witness to Jesus as the Christ are the authoritative texts. As authoritative, these texts are the principal means by which the contemporary Christian's faith in Jesus Christ is tested for its fundamental fidelity to the originating Christian witness to Jesus Christ. Indeed, it may be linguistically preferable to call these texts the "apostolic writings," as they were originally named, in order to highlight the fact that the Christian New Testament is a text of the witness to Jesus Christ of the original "apostolic" communities.

However, to affirm the central role of these texts is also to acknowledge a new Christian hermeneutical question, namely, where within the pluralism of texts and genres of the New Testament may we find the central Christian construal of this Jesus as the Christ and thereby the central Christian construal of God, self, history, and nature? Even the confession "We believe in Jesus Christ with the apostles" is, after all, properly in the genre of confession — and thereby abstracted from the diversity of New Testament Christologies to affirm their unity amidst that diversity. The confession, in sum, is a legitimate abstraction but is not an explicitly New Testament confession. Nor, for that matter, is confession the principal New Testament genre. Here, I believe, the rediscovery of narrative in contemporary Christian thought shows its true promise.

For the central genre for the original communities' self-interpretation is gospel — a peculiar genre which unites proclamation, witness, and narrative. Amidst the diversity of narratives within the four Gospels and elsewhere in the New Testament, moreover, the passion-resurrection narratives are the principal ways by which the early Christian community renders its understanding of who this singular Jesus of Nazareth, proclaimed to be the Christ, is. It is a useful exaggeration to say that the four Gospels are four passion narratives with extended and different introductions.

The reason why this statement is an exaggeration is that the introductions are more accurately described as different genres which construe the common narrative differently. There is, to be sure, a notable difference between the genre of apocalyptic drama employed by Mark, the genre of realistic, history-like narrative employed by Luke, and the genre of narrative meditation employed by John. Those genres, as not merely taxonomic of meaning but productive of meaning, provide distinct renderings of the basically common passion narrative. Still, the reason why this is a useful exaggeration may also be noted: the passion narratives and their relatively history-like, realistic character (Hans Frei) — despite their otherwise important differences — are the common Christian narrative. If one wants to know who Jesus Christ is for Christians, the passion narratives are the place to look. For there one finds in realistic and history-like fashion the central Christian construal of who this Jesus confessed to be the Christ is and even why he and he alone is thus construed.

Through that rendering of his singular identity in that narrative, Christians also discover their principal clues as to who God is and who human beings are empowered to become. In sum, as H. Richard Niebuhr long ago discerned, the Christian construal of the self as disclosed in these narratives of Jesus Christ entails a belief in an agent with sufficient freedom to be responsible to the God therein disclosed and to others through the power of this Jesus the Christ. The Christian, as Christian, needs to affirm the self-as-responsible-agent and thereby be sufficiently free to act responsibly. For to be able to respond in and through Christ to

God and to the neighbor is also to affirm the freedom to be capable of such action. On this foundation, I believe, all the principal Christian theological interpretations of the self and its freedom rest. For despite their otherwise crucial differences, on "freedom and grace" or "predestination and freedom" or "bondage of the will," all Christians affirm the reality of a responsible and thereby meaningfully free agent who is understood, through and in Christ, as a now authentically free self.

And yet, as the inner-Christian disputes on the exact nature of the freedom of the self of the post-New Testament Christian traditions indicate, there are clearly further questions and further construals of the self's freedom in the Christian tradition. Consider the following list alone: Karl Rahner vs. Karl Barth, Schubert Ogden vs. Rudolf Bultmann, Calvinists vs. Arminians, Jansenists vs. Jesuits, Banez vs. Molina, Erasmus vs. Luther, Abelard vs. Bernard of Clairvaux—and behind them all, the early Augustine vs. the later Augustine. These familiar clashes are intensified in Christian thought by the theological understandings of the social-political character of human freedom before God in the liberation, political, and feminist theologians. It is important to insist that, however conflictual these inner-Christian antagonisms are, all of them assume these crucial facts: first, there is meaning to the word *freedom* for the Christian insofar as that word refers to some notion of personal agency and some sense of personal responsibility; second, the ground of that freedom, as Paul insisted, is, for the Christian, Jesus Christ; and third, the center of that freedom is the kind of agent disclosed by the narratives on the singular agency of this Jesus as the Christ.

But to affirm anew the central role of these grounding narratives on agency in the context of the history of inner-Christian conflict on the character of the agent-as-free is to note the final promise and problem of inner-Christian understandings of agency and freedom. The problem is this: the conflict is there from the very beginning of Christian self-interpretation. The problem is there, more exactly, not just in the obvious differences, noted by Luther, between the anthropology of the Epistle to James and that of the Paul of Romans and Galatians. The problem is also there in different readings of the common passion narrative in the four Gospels and even in the abbreviated narrative of Paul in

1 Corinthians. Yet this problem yields, I believe, a promise of complementarity rather than sheer conflict. For significantly different readings of the common passion narrative occur in the different Gospels. Mark's apocalyptic drama is, as Frank Kermode justly observes, more like a modernist narrative which is interruptive, multivoiced, and characterized by nonclosure. Mark is notably different from the consistently realistic, history-like character of Luke which, in turn, is different yet again from the oratorio-like rhythms of the signs and manifestations of God's glory in the meditative narrative of John.

Here, perhaps, we may find a clue that at least two different readings of the common narrative pervade the New Testament. In general terms, let us name these two readings "prophetic" and "mystical." We shall see below, when reading Freud and Lacan, a more exact rendering of these different rhetorics and readings. For the moment, it is sufficient to note that the prophetic reading highlights the notion of freedom as responsible agency. That highlighting, in our period, is best represented by the insistence on freedom as personal agency and responsibility to the historical struggle of the marginalized and the oppressed in liberation theologies. It finds its most natural New Testament reading in Luke-Acts, where the history-like narrative aids the insistence on Jesus' actions for the outcasts of society and the need for freedom as not merely private but political as well. It is true that when prophecy fails, apocalyptic takes over — as in Mark's apocalyptic drama with its radically interruptive narrative. Yet even here, as the political theology of J. B. Metz shows, apocalyptic need not mean a retreat from subjecthood and the struggle for freedom in this interruptive history. Rather, apocalyptic can also become — in Mark's use of apocalyptic, if not perhaps in Revelation — an amazing insistence on both God as *the* agent in history and the subject as commanded and empowered to act freely even in these desperate, apocalyptic times.

The alternative reading to the prophetic is equally clear. For in the Gospel of John, the meditative and mystical rereading of the narrative presents a new view of the self's freedom-in-love and God-as-love-manifesting-Godself in *the sign* Jesus Christ. Can a mystic properly read a prophetic text? The question arises as soon as one acknowledges John's rereading of the Synoptic narrative.

The same question recurs when the Wisdom tradition and the prophetic tradition give their different readings of the common narratives of the Hebrew Scripture.

The strong sense of agency in the prophetic interpretation of the common reading can be challenged by the loving, meditative self, in union with a loving God, as portrayed in John. But is this really the case? As both the Neoplatonist Logos theologies and the love-mystics sensed, in John a new sense of freedom-as-love becomes a new possibility for human understanding. Neither the Christian prophet nor the mystic can live easily with one another. And yet, as many liberation, political, and feminist theologians now insist, only a mystical-prophetic construal of Christian freedom can suffice. Without the prophetic, the struggle for justice and freedom in the historical-political world can too soon be lost in mere privacy. Without the mystical insistence on love, the spiritual power of the righteous struggle for justice is always in danger of lapsing into mere self-righteousness and spiritual exhaustion.

The question of freedom for the Christian, therefore, is the fuller character of the free agent disclosed by the narrative of Jesus Christ, read anew in both prophetic and mystical ways. The ego in its alluring and illusory freedom is gone; the limited but real freedom of the subject-as-agent-in-process has occurred. But to shift to this modern vocabulary is also to suggest that perhaps this Christian interpretation of the self's freedom may also illuminate other rhetorics of freedom — perhaps even the contrasting rhetorics of Freud and Lacan.

III. THE PROPHET AND THE MYSTIC ON FREEDOM: FREUD AND LACAN

Religious languages arrive in two basic forms: the rhetoric of the prophet and the rhetoric of the mystic. First, the prophet: the prophet hears a word that is not her or his own. It is Other. It disrupts consciousness, actions, deliberations. It demands expression through the prophet. The prophet is not his own person; something else speaks here. Only on behalf of that Other may the prophet presume to speak her warnings, interruptive proclamations, predictions, and promises. Driven by a perfection language needing god-terms to disclose this Other who speaks through the prophet, she or he cannot but speak. The others ordinarily do not want to listen. But if matters get bad enough, as they usually do, others may begin to listen: first to the puzzling words of the Other in those words, then to the word of that Other in themselves. Some listen, some come for help, some are healed. Their healing will rarely prove a full recovery but, like Peter Brown's Augustine or Freud's Dora, more like a continuous convalescence. For consolation from all sorrow they must go elsewhere—to those who deny the Other. For the rhetoric of the prophet can only listen and help them hear the words of the Other in themselves.

Prophets have good reason to be discouraged about how few will listen. "Let those who have ears to hear, hear" is not a ringing assurance of success. Sometimes the prophets reflect their own fury at this Other who insists on speaking in them: witness the lamentations of Jeremiah and many of the letters of Freud. At other times this fury will disclose itself in the gaps, the fissures, the repressions of the prophets' own too-clear prose. At still other times, the prophets will yield to more reflective moods. They will face the fact that people seem to demand, not a word of the Other, but a consolation that cannot be given. They will note that the prophetic word is also "rotten with perfection." Ecclesiastes, that oddest of biblical books, is rhetorically that kind of work; so is *Civilization and Its Discontents*.

Freud was not a conquistador. His rhetoric was that of a prophet. Through his rods—as clear, definite, and, at the same time, self-interruptive as those of Amos—some Other spoke. Like all prophets, he would not let his prose indulge itself in the obscure and bizarre allegories of an apocalypticist or the weird, uncanny obfuscations of the mystic. He needed words that allowed the unconscious to speak and words persuasive enough to entice others to listen to that Other. But only clear, everyday words rendered with classic humanist restraint could allow that Other to be heard in such manner that others might hear and be persuaded. Freud called his god-term Logos—not mystery, not Other, not law. He called his discipline scientific. Science was for him, as for most in his period, the longed-for language of perfection after the languages of art, religion, and myth had failed. He often wanted to believe that his rhetoric, too, was purely scientific. Happily, it was something else: a rhetoric of corrigibility, clarity, seeking for evidence, that does indeed resemble science, but also a prose whose subtlety and restraint resembles Goethe. Both scientific and humanist, Freud's prose was finally an interruptive one—constantly interrupted, even disrupted, by the voice of the Other. By trying to render that subversive reality of the unconscious into seemingly scientific and humanist prose, Freud's powerful prophetic rhetoric challenged the ordinary prose of science and humanism alike as surely as the classic prophets' rhetoric, however clear and definite, smashed against the idols of the people. The prose becomes more and more polyvalent as it turns upon others and itself through the strange stories it narrates so well and the even stranger fissures and lapses it harbors within its own definiteness.

Finally, every word, including every word about words, becomes not merely ambiguous and polyvalent, but overdetermined and disseminating. The very material reality of these words of the Other invades all words—even the scientific words of Freud, the humanistic prose, the care and search for clarity and harmony. In that sense, Freud's persuasive prophetic rhetoric becomes, in his greatest texts, something like a kabbalistic palimpsest filled with words whose very materiality is the central clue to the revealing and concealing of the Other-in-words.

Mystical religious discourse is startlingly different from prophetic discourse. Both are driven by an impulse toward perfection in their words about the Word. Both seem driven by an Other who speaks. For the prophet, the Other is Word acknowledged in a word of proclamation ("Thus says the Lord") that disrupts the prophet's own consciousness and disseminates the ego and its illusory freedom. For the prophet is not her or his own person. The prophet, as responsible to the *fascinans et tremendum* power of the Word, must become a new self, freed by responsibility to others, to history, to the cosmos, because made responsible by the Other-as-Word. Only by losing the self can a new free self be gained. The Word must remain Other or else the Other in the new free responsible self cannot speak. The great Western monotheistic traditions (Judaism, Christianity, Islam) live by this prophetic rhetoric about the one God and the newly unified, responsible, othered self.

Mystics in prophetic traditions always have problems. Unless they are very cautious in their marginalized place, some prophet will accuse them of betrayal. Where is the God of the prophets in the Godhead-beyond-God of Meister Eckhart? Where are the energetics of Freud's unconscious in the linguistic unconscious of Lacan? Where is the radically monotheistic God and the free, responsible self in the apophatic Jewish, Christian, and Muslim mystics? Where is Freud's god Logos and where is the ego and its freedom in the uncontrollable prose and the unnerving tropes of Lacan? Have the Western apophatic mystics betrayed the prophets for Neoplatonism? Has Lacan betrayed Freud for Hegel and Heidegger?

At first, it may seem that monotheism is still honored by the mystics and a scientific Logos is honored by Lacan. For the mystic will try to reduce the world portrayed in the Bible to its most basic elements — God, world, soul — in order to observe their structural relationships. Mystics almost always have some basic grammar as their first move. Even Buddhists have the language of "dependent originations." Even Eckhart possesses a highly peculiar grammar of analogy. Lacan will also pay his tribute to structural relationships as his first move. Indeed, he will insist that only Saussure's linguistics can render scientific the discovery of the unconscious — an unconscious, of course, structured like a language. Every apophatic mystic in the monotheistic prophetic traditions will answer critics in much the same way: unfortunately, the prophets who wrote our sacred texts did not have available to them a grammar of the structural relationships of God-world-soul; fortunately, this grammar is now available to interpret the text correctly.

If the grammatical-structuralist move is the only move that the mystic makes, then all may be well — as the love-mystics hoped, as religious metaphysicians like Aquinas insist, as the Jungians with their strangely morphological if not structuralist archetypes believe, as all structuralists, from Saussure to Levi-Strauss, find sufficient.

But what if a second move is made? What if the apophatic element in mystical discourse takes a radical turn? Then, as in Pseudo-Dionysius, Erigena, and Eckhart, the basic structural elements of God-world-soul dissolve into one another and become self-negating. Eckhart's paradoxical "I pray to God to save me from God" is no prophetic rhetoric of humble submission. He is rather apophatically moving. But where? Perhaps into a radical mystical rhetoric of the Other, the "Godhead beyond" the prophets' God? When Eckhart proclaims a vision of "Leben ohne Warum" as a model for the self which is no-self, he is as far from the free responsible self of the prophets as he is from the agapic-erotic self of the Christian love-mystics. When Lacan informs us that the unconscious is structured like a language—only then to insist that there is no unitary sign, since the signifiers and not the signifieds rule—we are far, indeed, from the "sign" of Saussure. We are somewhere else—perhaps in the discourse of the Other? Perhaps in the apophatic excess of *jouissance*? Surely not in the all-too-free ego of ego-psychology.

Like Eckhart with his strange appeals to the orthodox analogical rhetoric of his fellow Dominican, Thomas Aquinas, Luther will also occasionally appeal to more orthodox views of the Other. Hence Lacan will appeal to the dialectical rhetoric of the Other in that strangest of orthodox Lutherans, Hegel, and the rhetorical poetics on "Language Speaks" in that oddest of post-Catholic Catholics, Heidegger. In Lacan's rhetoric there speaks, it seems, not only the Unconscious but the Other of the two most significant Greek Christians of modernity—the Protestant Hegel and the Catholic Heidegger. Both of them, after all, often read as gnomically as Eckhart, whom they both respected. Both of them also wanted an end to "theism" and "atheism" alike in favor of an Other who is finally allowed to speak. Both wanted new understandings of freedom beyond empiricism and rationalism. The orthodox psychoanalytic institutions may expel Lacan as firmly as the papal commission at Avignon condemned certain propositions of Eckhart. Yet both would continue to insist on their higher orthodoxy.

For them, only the mystic understands what the prophet really meant, for only the mystic knows both the basic structure of the whole and its radically destructuring actuality. Only the mystic knows the true freedom of the prophet.

But even the mystic may eventually find it necessary to adopt a prophetic rhetoric and proclaim the word of the Other. Otherwise, the others in their secure institutions will trivialize and reify the words of the Other once again. If necessary, prophetic actions may follow. Leaving the official institution, opening a new one, closing it, and starting again is an all-too-familiar prophetic activity. The careers of Eckhart and Lacan are often as uncannily parallel as their apophatic rhetorics. Neither was interested in either "theism" or "atheism," or in the usual understandings of freedom. That quarrel they freely left to those who did not understand the Other at all. They wanted *jouissance* and the uncanny tropes familiar in the authentic speech of the Other.

The question, "Does Lacan interpret Freud correctly?" therefore bears remarkable resemblance to the question, "Does the apophatic mystic interpret the prophetic text correctly?" Despite the decrees of Avignon, the case of Eckhart is still open; so is the case of Lacan. If the prophetic rhetoric needing interpretation is itself also a speech of the Other, it also becomes mystical rhetoric. Then the chances are reasonably good that a mystical interpretation of freedom may take hold. And if the mystic, however reluctantly, is forced into a prophetic role, with its insistence on free action, the chances are even better. But neither the theist nor the atheist, neither the empiricist nor the rationalist, need enter this new debate on freedom. The debate between the prophet and the mystic is like the debate between Luther and Erasmus. It is a rhetoric of the Other and the Other's freedom in relation to the self-in-process.

4
Freedom, Tolerance, and Puritan Commitment
ROBERT C. NEVILLE

I. THE PRINCIPLE OF UNIVERSAL PUBLIC RESPONSIBILITY

THE PRINCIPLE OF UNIVERSAL public responsibility, stated briefly, is that everyone in a social group is regularly responsible for all the group's public obligations. This principle stands in obvious contrast to the parallel assumption underlying the liberal tradition, namely, that any personal responsibility for the public good derives from the social contract, and that apart from the contract one is responsible only for one's private interests. When the social contract breaks down, liberalism assumes that obligation to the public good evaporates, and only private interests remain. The principle of universal public responsibility, deriving from the Puritan sensibility that preceded the rise of British liberalism, says, on the contrary, that when the social contract breaks down, primary responsibility returns to everyone, subject to certain qualifications.[1]

The principle of universal public responsibility asserts that in the state of nature everyone is responsible for all public goods of the group, whereas in the state of civil society that responsibility is divided and assigned artificially to special agents as defined by the contract or laws and customs. Privacy and freedom from public responsibility thus are artifacts of civil society, according to the principle of universal public responsibility. When the working forms of civil society break down or are in jeopardy, the privileges of privacy and freedom from public responsibility take second place. Primary responsibility is to public obligations. Because privacy, leisure, and attendant freedoms from having to attend to all public obligations are great goods, there is a powerful motivation to sustain and improve socially constructed orders. Yet the bite of the principle of universal public responsibility comes when society is in trouble. Instead of a collapse into an amoral chaos with little or no public responsibility—the implication of the liberal assumption—the principle of universal public responsibility points out the activated responsibility of everyone for the good of the social group as a whole. Although I do not intend to justify this principle here, I do want to explain it somewhat in order to express important concerns about its implications for freedom, tolerance, and commitment.[2]

1. The first point to note is that the principle assumes that nature and society contain real goods that can be discerned and related to possible action in order to be secured. This assumption has not been common in the modern era. The liberal contractarian theory from Hobbes and Locke to Rawls has assumed on the contrary that there are no real goods that can be known and pursued and has turned instead to a polity based on human wants and interests.[3] Indeed, the very strategy of placing responsibility exclusively within the social contract arises from the assumption that public goods are constructions resulting from agreements about how to pursue personal wants and interests. The liberal assumption about the value-neutrality of nature and society conforms to other metaphysical assumptions of the mathematical science of the modern era about the separation of facts and values.[4] There are many reasons to dispute that liberal assumption, but I will not engage them here.[5]

2. The second point in explaining the principle of universal public responsibility concerns the definitions of social good and public obligation. If goods are real and discernible, the content of the social good is of course an empirical matter. Most social goods are negative—for instance, the preservation of the peace, the alleviation of suffering, pain, hunger, oppression by others, and the like. Yet many social goods are positive, such as privacy and leisure for personal excellence, enjoyment of the fruits of the earth, the development of various human relationships, the arts and other

benefits of civilization, and a spiritual attunement to the earth and ultimate things. Then there are the various social institutions that are good because they secure or foster the others, for example, educational, judicial, religious, communal, and athletic institutions.

What makes these goods social rather than merely personal is that their achievement by some people benefits the rest. The key to this is the web of interconnections in social causation, interconnections with a wide variety of forms.[6] In a crude sense, the social group benefits from the health and security of individual members because they then can make their own contributions to the group, as better producers of food, goods, and services, nurturers and teachers of the young, warriors, and the like. Jefferson and others have made these interconnections more sophisticated in their argument for universal education: a democratic nation needs an educated citizenry. Deeper kinds of interconnection are revealed in empathy and sympathy for the experience of others. Starving people in Ethiopia, tortured people in totalitarian jails, all diminish us who are well-fed and free.

The social goods are obligations because their worthiness demands that something should be done, or abstained from, in order to achieve, secure, or protect them, other things being equal. The mere normativeness of social goods, however, only determines the public obligation that something should be done about them. "Someone should do something about that!" It does not determine who has the obligation. I distinguish public obligation, which is normative and general, from personal responsibility, which is a subject being under an obligation. To be responsible is to have one's moral character determined in part by an obligation. Liberalism can recognize general public obligations, but it relates those to individuals whose responsibility it is to fulfill them only by means of the social contract. Therefore, when the social contract goes seriously awry, all the then-obvious public obligations such as keeping the peace and securing the economy may fail to have anyone responsible for them. The principle of universal public responsibility says that precisely because of membership in the social group, all individuals, with certain qualifications, have responsibility for all social obligations. Liberal polity would be satisfactory only when everything is copasetic; such a time has not yet come. The principle of universal public responsibility addresses the situation when at least some people are ill served by the obtaining social structures. That time has always been with us.

3. The third point is the qualification to universal responsibility. There are two kinds of qualifications that can deactivate, as it were, all or part of a person's responsibilities to the public good: natural disabilities and social limitations. Natural disabilities are being too young or old, having disabling trauma or defects of birth or disease, being incompetent or removed from the action in ways that could not have been helped by planning or preparing differently earlier, and the like. Lurking behind all these natural disabilities is the primary responsibility to be ready for responsibility if at all possible.

Social limitations are the array of arrangements that divide up responsibilities to make culture efficient, finitely teachable, and capable of achieving more goods and avoiding more evils by virtue of cooperation and division of labor. A wholly unorganized society, with everyone attempting to fulfill all social obligations, would be total chaos.[7] All societies in their traditions and living cultures have social roles for rearing children, for attending to economic matters, to domestic chores, to defense and peace, for settling disputes, and the rest. I am not suggesting that the intentionality behind the development of social roles is for the sake of efficiency in fulfilling social obligations. On the contrary, the intentionality in most societies is part of the overall culture whose center is often religious or patriotic. Yet the division of labor regarding the social goods is what relieves each individual of having activated responsibility for all of them. By reason of whatever intentionality, most people have deactivated responsibility for most public obligations, usually on the condition that they have activated responsibility for certain specific responsibilities, often those for which they are specially fit or trained, and in the fulfillment of those few responsibilities act as surrogates for others.

Civilized societies do not divide labor exclusively according to inherited cultural roles. In addition there are explicit social constructs of leadership and other institutions for managing social organization itself, the matters of government, polity, and law on which the early contract theorists focused. Most issues of channeling responsibility for public obligations concern these explicit social constructs. And they are the ones that so often go wrong, so that the responsibilities they are supposed to handle in fact revert back to everyone.

4. The principle of universal public responsibility defines the social group as the causal interactions of people with one another, usually through the joint manipulation of material and cultural processes. The group is more or less tight according to the kind and density of the causal social interactions. With a few exceptions, the social group in our time is worldwide in many important respects. The divisions of people into separate nations, or separate language and cultural groups, are, among other things, divisions of labor, and their legitimacy needs to be tempered by judgments about whether they serve the achievement of the public social good. To the extent that nationalism, say, inhibits rather than promotes the worldwide social good, it is a detriment to the fulfillment of each person's responsibility. Because of the global network of social interactions, the group whose good most of us are responsible for seeking is a worldwide community. The goods of the worldwide community that provide universal public obligations are those having to do with the causal processes which constitute the worldwide community. There is a worldwide economic system, for instance, and in economic terms each individual has global responsibilities; there is no worldwide ethnic culture, and therefore no one has responsibilities for the good of all ethnic groups as such.

Now I am able to formulate the special concerns of this essay. What are the implications for social polity which flow from the principle of universal public responsibility? I have questions about three implications. What kind of social commitment is required to exercise universal responsibility? How can that commitment be prevented from overreaching itself so that one person takes it to be a personal responsibility to coerce another person to conform to the first person's definition of responsibility? Is there a sense of freedom that is native to universal public responsibility, or is freedom reduced to artificial protections against having to fulfill all responsibilities? These are the topics of Puritan commitment, tolerance, and freedom.

II. PURITAN COMMITMENT

In contrast to the liberal conception of atomic individualism, the principle of universal public responsibility implies that people ideally are individuated through fulfilling their connections with the things that have normative bearing on their lives. That is, people are individuated by being responsible for the particular context in which they relate to the universal range of obligations. And they are individuated ideally by the extent to which they fulfill those responsibilities. The modes and degrees to which people positively address their responsibilities give individuating content to life. The more tied in to the context in normative ways, the more one's individuality is fulfilled. This is to say, individuation comes with commitment to the normative tasks of one's context, and through that context to the normative tasks of the social group. This may be called the corollary of individuation through commitment.

It might seem that this is the wrong inference to draw from the principle of universal public responsibility. For, if everyone is responsible for all public obligations, except insofar as a socially constructed division of responsibility deactivates some responsibilities, then isn't everyone the same as far as responsibilities go? And then the contextual differences between people would be relatively trivial except insofar as they coincide with the social division of responsibilities. So whereas liberal polity assumes that people are essentially different because of their different contexts, and only contractually united in a system of responsibilities, the principle of universal public responsibility seems to trivialize the differences of context.

To answer this objection we need to remember that the keystone of the principle of universal public responsibility is the network of causal social relations by virtue of which individuals participate in a social group and in the group's activities regarding interactions with material and cultural processes. Involvement in the network is what transforms a general social obligation into the personal responsibility of individuals. The network of social processes is historically, geographically, and personally particular. Each person is particularly defined by the diverse implications of the network for the various positions the person occupies. If there were no responsibility involved, we might say that the person is individuated only as the particular unique congeries of all the network's implications for the person's positions. But since many of those implications place the person in relation to social goods that require particular responsibilities, the person is not just a complex set of roles but a partially self-creating or affirming individual. It is through responsibility for particular things, and commitment to fulfilling those responsibilities, that one becomes an individual in the full sense. Being responsible gives one a moral soul, and how one fulfills those responsibilities, for better or worse, gives one a moral character.

The particularity of one's individuality comes from the fact that responsibilities are always contextual. One is responsible for the more general social obligations—keeping the peace, voting for governmental leaders, paying taxes, and so forth—because one's particular social context is causally connected with those general obligations. One also has more proximate responsibilities to one's job, local community, religious and civic organizations, family, and so forth. Proximate responsibilities are not merely means for fulfilling more general ones, nor are the general responsibilities for the sake of supporting the proximate affairs; there is a reality to social obligation at all levels of generality. Yet it is through the causal structures connecting proximate affairs with more general ones that all individuals have responsibilities for the most general obligations.

In good times there is a division of responsibility such that dealing with proximate responsibilities virtually fulfills all one's activated responsibilities save those served through tokens such as taxes. In these good times, government responsibility is activated only for officials for whom holding office is a proximate responsibility. But bad times reactivate people's responsibilities for a wide range of goods, many far from their local context. The leisure of deactivated responsibilities is diminished. Yet the obligatoriness of even the most remote and general social good falls upon the diverse individuals because of the diverse particular ways in which the context of each of them is networked with the larger group. One is a citizen in general and a parent of particular children, both at once with concomitant responsibilities; yet the reason both provide responsibilities is that they are causally connected.

The virtue arising from recognition of this ground of responsibility is commitment to the good of the social group, that is, commitment to fulfilling responsibilities in all the contexts in which one participates, general and proximate. Because that commitment is the substance of one's pursuit of moral responsibilities, it is the trait that underlies moral character. Commitments are always particular because even general responsibilities, such as for peace in the world, are always mediated by the particularities of more proximate contexts that bear their own responsibilities.

The people who best recognized the individuating function of commitment were the early Puritans. They understood that each person is an individual in the eyes of God, with an individual salvation to be fulfilled by relating rightly to every part of the person's social context — to family, community, work, and country. Even though many of the Puritans entertained a deterministic metaphysics, they thoroughly understood that salvation meant changing bad laws and social conditions that made life hard for people. Their social revolution was for the sake of improving the lot of all the individuals whose salvation was at stake.

But then their revolution was a terror: bloody, coercive, and utterly contradictory in effect to the aim of bringing a kingdom of God on earth. Nearly everyone in England sighed with relief when the restoration of Charles II brought in moral relaxation and liberal tolerance. We have only to remember the Salem witch trials, the excesses of the Great Awakening, or the potential tyranny of the so-called Moral Majority, to know that in certain crucial respects, Puritanism is a very bad thing. The Puritans seemed better suited to being critics safely kept out of office. What is wrong with Puritan commitment?

III. TOLERANCE

The formal difficulty with Puritan commitment can be stated rather simply. If I am responsible for everything, then I am responsible for seeing that you fulfill your responsibilities. If that merely meant that I would help you, there would be only a grateful situation. But it can also mean that I must define your responsibilities because they are part of my responsibilities. The usual existential implication of the Puritan polity was that everyone is in authority over everyone else. Since this cannot work, power politics, mediated in the Puritans' case by a religious ideology, decides whose authority is really authoritative. The authoritative authorities then are responsible not only for the social good but for the moral character of everyone else. In small part, the difficulty here is with knowledge of the good. Although I believe that there are natural goods and that they can be discerned, their discernment is difficult and partial. Even with the best of will, people can genuinely disagree about what is obligatory and what to do about it. But individuals in disagreement can recognize that they must refrain from insisting on their opinions until the issues of moral discernment have been clarified enough for cooperative responsible activity to be undertaken. The chief difficulty is not disagreement in knowledge but disagreement in will or conscience. Conscientious Puritans believed they must insist upon their conscience.

So the way out of the dilemma is to deny social authority in its strong sense altogether. And the way to make that denial is to recur to a valid insight of both Puritanism and liberalism, namely, that each person is the responsible author of his or her own actions and influences. The seat of responsibility is in the individual subject, just as the content of responsibility is in the objective goods that are obligatory to serve. The principle of universal public responsibility joins the objective content of obligation to the subjective seat of responsibility. It implies that one person cannot, logically, spiritually, or metaphysically, exercise another's responsibility. Since the excellence of individuation involved in developing one's virtues in fulfilling responsibility is one of the greatest goods encountered in civilized experience, East and West, there is a deep and pervasive social obligation on everyone to encourage the development of responsibility in others. Negatively put, the abridgment of someone else's responsibility is a deep evil. More precisely stated, the abridgment of someone else's responsibility, when that person is indeed capable of being responsible, is merely violence against that person; it cannot be a substitute proxy for that person's responsibility.

The moral is that tolerance is a fundamental political virtue. Tolerance has primary and secondary levels. At the primary level tolerance is the explicit allowing of space for other people to engage their responsibilities, and to achieve a moral character appropriate to their success or failure at that engagement. At secondary levels tolerance is adjusting to the ways, perhaps idiosyncratic, inefficient, and costly to others, by which others approach or avoid their responsibilities. Secondary tolerance is putting up with ways of life or approaches to problems we might never approve for ourselves, for the sake of allowing others to engage their obligations on their own responsibility. Contrary to the practice of the Puritans, therefore, the principle of universal public responsibility enjoins the practice of tolerance at both levels. Tolerance is not a minor virtue, like politeness. It is a fundamental political virtue arising from recognition of the nature of responsibility as subjectively seated in responsible individuals.

There are at least three circumstances in which we generally recognize that tolerance comes in conflict with other obligations: circumstances of emergency, cooperation, and sin.

In circumstances of emergency one or more persons can perceive that the tolerance of another person's secondary ways of exercising responsibility, or even primary space to act responsibly, will lead to disastrous results. We tolerate Grandma's slow, cautious driving, for to deprive her of it would be severely to limit her life options; but we grab the wheel when she is about to make a stupid mistake. When a community's safety is threatened by invaders, we limit tolerance by conscription of human and material resources according to the plans of leaders. Even in these cases, however, it is an empirical matter whether the danger in continued tolerance outweighs the cost of denying the others the possibility of pursuing their responsibility in primary or secondary ways. When President Reagan was shot and Secretary of State Haig said, "I am in charge here," it was deadly wrong of him to undermine the constitutional authority of Vice-President Bush, even if it be true that Haig would be far better than Bush in a real emergency. When Admiral Poindexter and Lieutenant Colonel North thought that the legal political process would lead to a disastrous foreign policy, and instituted an illegal process of undercover government, they were mistaken to believe that their emergency outweighed the value of constitutional government. But we can imagine scenarios in which the reverse judgments might be made, when the legal government simply fails its obligations and when Grandma really ought to be prevented from driving, for her own sake and the safety of others. The judgment of when an emergency obtains that justifies limiting tolerance is the moral responsibility of each participant in the affair, and that judgment may turn out in retrospect to be mistaken, or everlastingly controversial. In a well-ordered society, with a finely tuned system of allocating activated responsibilities for determining when such an emergency obtains, there is a due process for making the determining decision. We can be satisfied in such a society that the "right" decision is simply what the Supreme Court, or the President, or the Congress decides. But some emergencies of large scale call that due process into question. In no circumstance does the judgment that an emergency obtains fail to be the responsibility of the participants, with moral consequences for all.

The need for cooperation is a circumstance that can limit tolerance, as when all hands are needed to row the boat out of danger. On a superficial level, cooperation can be understood pragmatically. Many of the fundamental obligations of a society require cooperation, and hence a tailoring of ways of addressing responsibilities to the patterns of the cooperative enterprise. In a society with automobile traffic, traffic laws appropriately limit driving practices. In a society with a need for defense, welfare entitlements, and the rest, tolerance of how individuals spend their money is appropriately limited by taxation and contracts.

On a more fundamental level, however, cooperation is intrinsic to the human condition because much of what makes us human is the use of signs and meaningful actions and gestures. Most of what we do is significant, and most of what we are is the result of attaining to the ability to participate in the social system of significant things. Therefore, we are already cooperative in our being and practices, and bare participation in the social system itself is a massive qualification of what otherwise might be conceived as unlimited tolerance. Because a high degree of cooperation is already assumed by the mere fact of participation in the social system, tolerance has come to mean tolerance of deviations from the normal expectations and ways of interpreting and sending social messages. Tolerance is of eccentricity. To admit that tolerance involves special cases of making room for eccentricity is to acknowledge that the potential field of tolerable ways of life has already been severely limited by elementary participation in the social system.

The circumstance I call *sin* is the greatest test of tolerance. By sin I here mean, not the whole Puritan Christian doctrine of original fall and corruption of mind and will, but the simple fact that nearly everyone sometimes, and some people much of the time, act in ways that deliberately deny their responsibility. The problem is not that they are klutzes, or that their way of fulfilling responsibilities is unnecessarily costly to the rest of us; the problem is that they do evil, that they act so as to undermine their own responsibilities and interrupt the means by which we attend to ours. All too often, the sinner is ourselves. Can sin be tolerated? The Puritan said no, and from this judgment stemmed the terror of Puritan authoritarianism. Yet I think the answer must be yes, sin must be tolerated, although it is everyone's responsibility to ameliorate the public consequences of sin as much as possible, and to prevent them where predictable. Society should demand of people a minimal degree of responsible behavior — not stealing, murdering, raping, or committing mayhem — as a condition for admitting them to various privileges of social participation such as the right to socialize with others or be around other people's property. Beyond punishment for crimes, punishment that respects the responsibility of the perpetrator, society can protect itself against future criminal action if it has very good reason to believe the person cannot act responsibly. This of course requires scrupulous attention to due process, to guard against special interest in the judgment about the nature of crime and in the characterization of the alleged criminal's responsibility. We also need to be alert to the deficiencies of due process itself that might come from its control by special interests. In addition, we must recognize, as Martin Luther King, Jr., argued, that sometimes responsibility for the public good obliges people to disobey a social structure that seriously inhibits their pursuit of responsibility; this is not sin in any sense but a courageous attention to responsibility. In general, the application of the notion of tolerance in circumstances of sin is to tolerate the sinner because evil is rewarded in an appropriate moral character but not to tolerate certain rights of participation in society that need to be earned by demonstrated responsible behavior. Persons have no right to the fruits of sinful action.

IV. FREEDOM

Either as an individual virtue or as generalized into social policy, tolerance is a negative good. It is fundamental to the principle of universal public responsibility because it is an essential corrective to the corollary of individuation through commitment. Each person's commitment must be tolerant of the other's commitment, or failure of commitment, because not to be tolerant is to mistake the individual subjective seat of responsibility.

Beyond tolerance, is there no positive virtue of freedom, as suggested in the topic of this group of essays? I believe there is, though it is a complex ideal with many dimensions. Let me close by mentioning four dimensions: political freedom, personal freedom, social freedom, and spiritual freedom.

1. The heart of political freedom, I believe, is the obverse of tolerance. That is, no person or government can logically or metaphysically have the right to abridge a person's authorship or responsibility for what the person is and does. Positively put, governments and people ought to acknowledge the inalienability of authorship and responsibility. The reason for this is not the liberal one, that people are free unless there is a contractually valid law inhibiting that freedom. It is rather the recognition that people are naturally responsible for the public good, and that their authority for their own actions is inalienably their own. Enjoyment of political freedom in this sense does not mean that one's actions or liberties cannot be curtailed for the public good, if the needs of the social good so demand. On the other hand, what the structures of society determine in the matter might be mistaken. The public good might not require the curtailment of the actions in question.

The political legitimacy of regulating individuals' actions for the public good is not identical with the content of what the political structure decides. A political decision might well be an illegitimate one, not justified by the needs of the public good. Procedural legitimacy does not guarantee moral or even political legitimacy in the larger sense. A totalitarian government that tortures its enemies according to a clear law is not politically or morally legitimate for all its due process. Political freedom, in the restricted sense I am using the term here, means the recognition of the subjective seat of responsibility and authorship of actions, and the respect for such actions unless the public good requires their inhibition.

2. The personal dimension of freedom, often confused with the political, consists of at least four dimensions. The first is freedom to act. Negatively, this means external liberty, not being inhibited in action by nature, society, or government. This sense of freedom is closely tied with political freedom. Positively, this aspect of personal freedom means capacity to act, which requires culture, training, education, experience, and practice, often specifically related to a field of action. This is the aspect of freedom that Hobbes, Spinoza, and Edwards focused upon. Secondly, personal freedom involves the ability to choose among alternatives. On the one hand this means having real options for choice, and on the other the capacity to make choices, a capacity again dependent upon knowledge, experience, and practice. Failure to have the freedom to choose among alternatives means that, despite the freedom to act, there is no special responsibility that can be assigned to the actor rather than the actor's antecedents. Responsibility requires that the actor as chooser make the crucial difference. The third aspect of personal freedom is the freedom to choose according to standards. Random choice can make the actor responsible but not morally responsible. The fourth aspect, closely related, is the freedom to criticize standards for choice and take responsibility for using the standards one does. This is responsive to Kant's discussion of the sense in which responsibility is giving oneself a law.

3. The personal dimension of freedom is abstract relative to actual life, and it needs to be understood in conjunction with the social dimension of freedom. This also has four dimensions: opportunity, social pluralism, integral social life, and political participation.

For freedom of opportunity, society needs to provide access to the media of social participation. It needs to make clear and available what might be valuable to people; and it needs to foster engagement with culture that turns a naked opportunity into a prized real option. Social pluralism is that aspect of society allowing space for privacy, for ways of doing things and fulfilling responsibility that are not preempted by the needs for conjoint action in the service of the public good. Only by organizing society with deactivated responsibilities and channeled activities is it possible to make room for the privacy that genuine creativity requires. Social freedom also requires a social structure that makes integral life possible. This is not problematic in a monolithic society denying privacy and social pluralism, but in a pluralistic society it is difficult to find individual integrity. Social freedom also requires avenues of participation by which people modify their social environment. Democracy is the great family of ideas about how to structure the governance of society so that people's responsibility to the public good is congruent with their powers of affecting social conditions. All aspects of the social dimension of freedom are important parts of the social good, and they constitute obligations for which individuals are responsible in various ways according to their particular contexts.[8]

The spiritual dimension of freedom has to do with the attainment of spiritual excellence or perfection. This has a negative side, freedom from sin, ignorance, or stain, and a positive side, the achievement of high levels of spiritual power and experience, which include the transformation and integration of other dimensions of freedom. The spiritual dimension of freedom is extraordinarily interesting in its own right, especially as it affects the notion of individuation discussed above.[9] But for the most part, with one exception, the spiritual dimensions of freedom are not internal to the political affairs governed by the principle of universal public responsibility. That one exception has to do with guilt.

By virtue of the principle of universal public responsibility, we have more responsibilities than we can possibly fulfill. Even if society were ordered with utter perfection, so that each person had responsibilities neatly in keeping with that person's powers, and each person fulfilled those responsibilities perfectly, and all social obligations were tied to individuals whose responsibility they were, the situation wouldn't last. Someone would be born when the stars were out of alignment, as Plato said, and the perfect social structure would be unprepared and thus dysfunctional. Or someone would sin, leaving a hole in the network of responsible actions.

The realistic situation is that much of the time we fail at the responsibilities we undertake and neglect responsibilities we hope are being cared for elsewhere. Even if we don't do that, others will, so that we are given new responsibilities. There is thus inevitable failure, and we, being subjectively responsible for it all, are guilty. Religions address that guilt or failure. In the Christian tradition, the belief that guilt is not our natural state is the sin of pride, the sin of thinking we are infinite and perfect like God. Redemption, or enlightenment, or the attainment of true sageliness, is the religious way to cope with the human condition brought to light by the principle of universal public responsibility.[10]

I have tried to defend a political principle that I believe cuts reality more nearly at its natural joints than the competing assumptions of the closely related liberal tradition. The principle of universal public responsibility emphasizes positive responsibility over individual freedom as the basis for justifying political orders. It points out that the true nature of human life is to be contextually and socially defined, and that virtue consists in commitment to fulfilling responsibilities to that context. The grave danger in this approach is its incipient authoritarianism, which can move as far as totalitarian terror. For this reason, an obligation to tolerance is intrinsic to the principle of universal public responsibility, for that obligation is commanded by the need to respect the fact that each person is subjectively responsible for the public good, responsible in ways that others cannot displace. Freedom, then, in its political, personal, social, and spiritual dimensions, especially the political and social, is an achievement of cultural order, and a great good we are obligated to serve. Freedom is not natural, like responsibility, but a product of civilization. No one needs to defend responsibility: we are responsible whether or not we accept the fact and attempt to do well by it. But freedom has been dearly bought and is in danger of decay. Its protection is the social good on which our own culture has pinned its identity and excellence.

NOTES

1. The principle of universal public responsibility does not occur in Puritan writings, so far as I know, but is a political principle I derive from the Puritan sensibility, or from the sensibility of some Puritans. On the Puritan sensibility see William Haller, *The Rise of Puritanism* (New York: Columbia University Press, 1930; Harper, 1957). By *Puritans* I mean

mainly those in Britain, the ones who lost out to, or became, liberals after the restoration of King Charles II. For an account of what happened after the collapse of English Puritanism, or rather after its disastrous success in the Protectorate of Cromwell, see Christopher Hill, *The Experience of Defeat: Milton and Some Contemporaries* (New York: Elisabeth Sifton Books/Viking, 1984). For a study of the continuity of Puritan and liberal cultures, see Edmund Leites, *The Puritan Conscience and Modern Sexuality* (New Haven, Conn.: Yale University Press, 1986). For a more elaborate discussion of the contemporary advantages and dangers of recurring to Puritan thought—scouting around liberalism, as it were—see Robert C. Neville, *The Puritan Smile* (Albany: State University of New York Press, 1987); see chaps. 8 and 9 for a more detailed discussion of authority and the distinction between the public and the private than is contained in this essay.

2. The political philosophy from which the principle of universal public responsibility comes is defended in Robert C. Neville, *The Cosmology of Freedom* (New Haven, Conn.: Yale University Press, 1974); and *The Puritan Smile*.

3. This remark is not entirely fair to Rawls. See his discussion of the good in *A Theory of Justice* (Cambridge, Mass.: Harvard University Press, 1971), chap. 7. Nevertheless, both his "thin" and "thick" theories of goodness have to do with rationality and subjective enjoyment or desire, not with the intrinsic value of things, or their worthiness to be enjoyed or desired. The intent of his contract theory is to make judgments of intrinsic goodness of natural and social things unnecessary; they are replaced by ingenious procedures and an analysis of rationality and desire.

4. For careful accounts of this see E. A. Burtt's classic, *The Metaphysical Foundations of Modern Science*, rev. ed. (Garden City, N.Y.: Doubleday Anchor, 1954); and Eugene M. Klaaren, *Religious Origins of Modern Science* (Grand Rapids, Mich.: Eerdmans, 1977).

5. See Robert C. Neville, *Reconstruction of Thinking* (Albany: State University of New York Press, 1981), chaps. 1-4; and *The Puritan Smile*.

6. For a brilliant philosophical analysis of social associations and connections, see Paul Weiss, *Toward a Perfected State* (Albany: State University of New York Press, 1986).

7. Perhaps the most serious attempt to envision such an unorganized state was made by the early Taoists. See Norman J. Girardot, *Myth and Meaning in Early Taoism: The Theme of Chaos (Hun-Tun)* (Berkeley: University of California Press, 1983).

8. See Neville, *The Cosmology of Freedom*, pts. 2 and 3, respectively.

9. On spiritual freedom see Robert C. Neville, *Soldier, Sage, Saint* (New York: Fordham University Press, 1978).

10. The discussion of the religious element of guilt is detailed in Neville, *The Puritan Smile*, chap. 10: "Responsibilities in Conflict."

PART II

Philosophies of Freedom

5
Freedom as Self-Determination
JOHN E. SMITH

FREEDOM INVOLVES TWO ISSUES: first, whether freedom is a reality, or some sort of illusion; second, the concrete meaning we have in mind when we attribute freedom to human beings. Obviously, the two issues cannot be discussed without reference to each other, for in order to determine whether something is a reality we shall have to have some idea of the something in question. It was in this vein that Kant, for example, spoke first of a *negative* freedom that is essentially a possibility or a capacity, and then went on to define a *positive* freedom that outlines the way in which this capacity is actualized.

There are obstacles, however, be they assumptions or prejudices, that in my view have stood in the way and prevented us from having a clear understanding of our subject. To begin with, there is the assumption that freedom stands in opposition to any sort of causal efficacy or restraint. This assumption seems obviously wrong because such freedom would necessarily be arbitrary and chaotic. Some form of determination as this act, and not that, must be an ingredient in any understanding of freedom. A second claim to be rejected is the view that self-determination is a disguised form of determinism, since presumably we can always show that the self in question is determined by the society and environmental factors, and hence that it forms but one more link in the chain. For the moment it is sufficient to say that this view depends on a distorted conception of what a self is. Closely connected with the previous point is another pitfall to be avoided, namely, the tendency, expressed in many ways by philosophers in the past, to carry over into the analysis of human agency and action ideas derived chiefly from our understanding of the nature of objects and the relations between them. This error has had disastrous consequences and is difficult to overcome, especially in view of the fact that many modern philosophers have supposed that relations themselves are supplied by the mind, leaving the world around us no more than a collection of things.

The truth is that when we reflect upon ourselves as human beings, and not as philosophers committed to supposedly superior views of things, we know that the agent or self is not an object in any ordinary sense — even if it can be made, as I prefer to call it, an *objective* of reflection. Here it appears that the philosophers of existence were somewhat misleading when they insisted that analysis or reflection about the self or subject *ipso facto* transformed it into an object. But surely the self no more becomes an object by becoming the focus of reflection than a number becomes a thing you can hold in your hand when it becomes the focus of reflection in discussions about the foundations of arithmetic. Actions are not to be accounted objects either, again, in any ordinary sense. Both are temporally extended events, related to the agent in ways unique to what we may call the activity situation. Hence, in order to consider the relations between an agent and its activity, relations essential to any discussion of freedom, it will be necessary to pay attention to the nature of self as agent and to see an act as an event in the ongoing biography of a person.

So much for some obstacles. Before taking up the positive task implied in the preceding discussion, something must be said about the theory of determinism, or what Peirce called the "doctrine of necessity." The reason for that is quite simple. If certain conceptions of universal determinism of a mechanical or quasi-mechanical sort are valid, it would make little, if any, sense even to begin to set forth a theory of freedom. Here I plan to make no excursion into the principle of indeterminacy, quantum mechanics, or Einstein's dislike of the dice-playing God. Rather, I will propose several philosophical considerations that make the world safe for freedom, if we can succeed in making sense of what it actually means once its possibility has been put on a sound footing.

A groundswell in modern philosophy, beginning with Kant but minus his two unconnected worlds of theoretical determinism and practical freedom, has made itself felt through Peirce, Bergson, James, Whitehead, and others in defense of the view that reality cannot be rightly understood without the ingredience of a mode of real possibility in the nature of things. It is extremely interesting that, despite great differences in their approach to the challenge of determinism, Peirce and James came to the same conclusion about the reality of possibility. Three basic considerations are relevant in this regard:

1. The argument that determinism — before the fact the only possible outcome was the *one* that *had* to happen — is a necessary postulate for the scientific enterprise is false. It not only begs the point at issue but remains in the end no more than a postulate. As Peirce pointed out, if one owes a debt of two hundred dollars it takes no effort at all to postulate the sum of two hundred dollars, except that the debt remains unpaid. What we want to know is whether determinism is true, not that we must conceive the world in this way in order to make way for science. The curious fact is that the deterministic universe once thought to be the mainstay of physics has migrated to psychology, in representatives like B. F. Skinner, where it serves to help overcome the deep-seated anxiety about whether psychology is scientific.

2. The mechanical model for understanding both natural processes and human development is inadequate and must not be taken as a paradigm. If by *mechanical* we mean a process in which there is exact repetition of a cycle that is also reversible, it is difficult to see how such a way of understanding could do justice both to organic processes and to human activity. If, for example, we consider a machine designed to stamp out nails from drawn wire, it is clear that the process must repeat itself exactly each time a nail is produced. There is no novelty or variety involved. The thousandth nail is to be the same as the first. But the most obvious fact about the domain of organisms, including human beings, is the presence of novelty, variety, creativity, and an increment of value that cannot be understood as a cycle that merely repeats itself. There is, moreover, a temporal asymmetry in organic development which is excluded by mechanical reversibility. Apart from the entertaining paradoxes of relativity physics, our experience is that we grow older, not younger; plants, insects, birds, and animals wax and wane in one direction as the cosmic process passes from the past through the present into the future. Peirce made

this point some three-quarters of a century ago when he argued, in connection with the theory of evolution, that the process cannot be mechanical in character precisely because of increasing heterogeneity in the natural order and the fact of variation among members of the species. How are these facts to be accounted for in terms of the exact repetition of a cycle that can have but one determinate outcome? As Peirce says, what is needed for understanding organic processes is a doctrine of real possibility according to which the following two opposed alternatives are both rejected; it is not true of any organic development that only one outcome can happen — the one that *had* to happen — nor is it true that anything you please may happen, for on that view we would do no more than replace determinism by chaos. The correct view is that in all these cases there is, before the fact, a range of real possibilities or alternative outcomes that allows for the element of real choice in human affairs.

One of the main reasons why possibility has been overlooked or even denied is found in the widespread belief in modern thought since Kant that only one mode of being is needed, namely, *existence*, or present, fully determinate, bare fact. But as the whole of Whitehead's thought shows, such a limited conception of what the world contains cannot possibly provide an adequate account of human development and of civilization. The mode of possibility is needed as an essential ingredient in the cosmic scheme. In the end, the reality of possibility is the anchor of freedom.

With these preliminary considerations in mind, we can approach more directly the conception of freedom as self-determination. The basic idea behind the doctrine is that the agent should possess the ability of self-determination. The agent should possess the ability to make self-conscious choices where several courses of action present themselves, along with the power to carry out the deed called for by the decision. Kant made this doctrine stand in opposition to heteronomy, wherein decision and action are determined by factors other than the self. Thus, for example, in the political application of the principle, law imposed by a tyrant places all those subject to it in the position of heteronomy, since no individual can see the law as an embodiment of his or her will, but only as the alien will of the tyrant.

Important as the distinction is, however, there are at least two reasons why we should not make autonomy and heteronomy into a knife-edge distinction, on the assumption that we know what belongs to the self as distinct from what is external. The first is that in the concrete situation of willing and acting there will necessarily be present factors, including some within the makeup of the agent, over which he or she has little or only quite limited control. My ability to be patient, for example, varies from time to time, and on some days it will bear more trying than on others. What degree of this ability belongs to me, and what is to be put down to external constraint? Are we to resolve the problem by identifying the self exclusively with factors over which it has total control? Kant could draw his distinction quite rigidly because he saw the agent solely in terms of will and practical reason and regarded freedom or autonomy as the dutiful willing of the moral law, all of which manages to omit much that is present in the actual self. Kant suffered the consequence of this omission by not being able to give an adequate account of action because he could not connect the noumenal and phenomenal selves, the self of freedom with the self that must bring about the act.

Secondly, the self is more inclusive than what we have come to call the will, and indeed wider than any of the traditional faculties that are supposed to constitute the self. Consider the making of a decision or, as we say, making up our minds. The very existence of a problem in this connection is due to our being of more than one mind. If we are deliberating about alternatives, we find ourselves having already invested an interest in more than one alternative, and making up our minds is not accomplished by the mind alone but by the withdrawal of interest and concern from all but one alternative. We must exercise reason in analyzing, comparing, and attempting to assess the merits of the alternatives, but that effort itself is made within a wider matrix of field of consciousness than the reflecting mind. Habits, tendencies, interests, and numerous other features in the ongoing life of the self will form part of the total reality, so that under no circumstances can we single out any one item and say, that is the self. Here we see the error of the Cartesian identification of the self with the mind.

There is a deeper reason, however, why no such identification is possible. The self does not have fully determinate boundaries, not because of any failure of knowledge but because it is a reality that cannot be regarded as something already all there. It is a dynamic system growing and developing into the future. The self is to some extent always in the making and, while it is at any given time thus far made, there is still more to come. It is precisely this indeterminacy with respect to the boundaries of the self that makes it difficult indeed to say what is *autos* or the self as autonomous and what is *heteros* or the self as externally determined. As we shall see, it is this fact that must figure largely in any attempt to make sense of the idea of freedom as self-determination.

Thus far I have been referring to the self as if it were something that we all understand. That, of course, is not true. We are familiar with the experience of being a self, but that alone does not provide us with a clear concept of what it is. Further, this familiarity may thwart our efforts to understand what and who we are. Pitfalls surround the familiar. Frustration comes from not being able to articulate what we are sure we must know by acquaintance. H. D. Lewis in his Gifford Lectures of some years ago referred to the "elusive self" as a major philosophical issue. That is a description that no one is likely to challenge. It used to be said that failure to resolve the problem of induction, supposedly the backbone of science, is the "scandal of philosophy." In my view, the elusive self is a far better candidate.

We use the word *I* constantly and invariably with a certain tender regard, but it is only with great difficulty that we are able to say what we mean. Here we confront the paradox that actually being something does not necessarily furnish us with a clear conception of what it is to be that something. Even Descartes with his *cogito* could claim to know *that* he is, while admitting that *what* he is is quite another matter and not to be read off, as it were, from the "I think" itself, unless, of course, we identify the two, and that is a mistake.

James pointed out in his *Psychology* that discussions of the self in early modern philosophy were dominated, on the one hand, by the Cartesian conception of the substantial ego and, on the other, by the Humean conception of the self as a "bundle of perceptions." For a number of reasons too extensive for treatment here, neither of these views can stand up to criticism based on actual experience. No one encounters the substantial self in experience, and this

I would maintain despite the fact that I believe that something more is involved in the awareness of "I think" than Russell's proposed reduction of it to "there are thoughts." The substantial self, moreover, poses a further problem, namely, that it is supposed to be a substrate underlying the stream of experience and is, as such, something identical and unchanging. It is, however, not possible to give an intelligible account of how this substrate is related to the temporal, changing, and ongoing course of the individual's experience as it unfolds. Hume's conception fares no better. Even if we allow, as I would, that we are unable to apprehend the self as a singular datum in reflection, the unifying element represented by the "bundle" is, in addition to being quite vague, too weak to sustain both the identity and the cumulative development or growth of a person. And how does a person develop a definite moral character through the exercise of freedom?

James and Royce, in different ways, were right to abandon both approaches and to strike out in another direction. The new attempt was to construe the self as a dynamic system of natural endowments — feelings, ideas, habits, purposes — unified by what I call a "center of intention" manifested through a dominant aim that persists over time and change and defines the individual in terms of what it means, or intends, to become and to be. Long before Sartre's conception of the existing individual as a project put forth under the aegis of an absolute freedom, Royce proposed to define the self as a meaningful course of events, a biography, or a special sort of history focused by a single agent, unified by an overarching purpose, to which the person is committed and through which he or she finds a guide for decision and action. Central to this way of envisaging the self is the pivotal fact that the self is not "given" to us as something inherited but is an achievement marked by will, determination, and effort. The similarity between this view and Sartre's is obvious, but there is a crucial difference between the two, and it points up an error that Royce avoided and Sartre did not. In Sartre's view, we are supposed to have what I like to call "free freedom," the capacity to project and create *ex nihilo*, as it were. For him, to acknowledge both the reality of the past and our natural constitution — what we already were and have now become — is *ipso facto* to become a victim of bad faith and a fugitive from freedom. Royce, by contrast, recognized the finite character of human freedom and took seriously the nature of the concrete self, something that is both richer and deeper than a pinpoint of freedom creating out of and into nothing. It is ironical that Sartre, the philosopher of existence and the critic of abstractions, should hold forth a fantastic conception of the self, admittedly shaped by the urgency of extreme circumstances, while Royce, the speculative idealist, should present a sober view much more in accord with the self as we know it. In any case, Royce was right to distinguish, within the boundaries of the self, between elements that, on the one hand, must be put down to what we have inherited — our capabilities, talents, habits, place in the social order, plus all the physical features we share with others in the environment — and, on the other, the will and purpose that belong to each of us uniquely and determine how we, in freedom, synthesize and direct these elements to form the one person we mean to be. We always have to work with much that we did not create of ourselves. Tillich called this the element of "fate" or destiny that cannot be expunged from human freedom. But we have an obligation and an ability to achieve the self we mean to be, this individual and no other. We are creatures of freedom but this does not mean that we *are* freedom.

Viewing the elusive self as a meaningful biography developing in time and centered by a dominant purpose seems to me the most fruitful idea. It most adequately captures the pervasive experience we have of being a self. When we say "I" as a subject and "me" as an object of reference, we do not mean that there is some definite entity that is or might become an object of perception. Nor do we mean merely a conception of ourselves that would include the generic features that are shareable with others and go to form the concept of selfhood as such. We mean, instead, our own ongoing life stretching over time and suffused both with an awareness of what we are trying to achieve and the person we are striving to be, but especially with the sense, in James's vivid phrase, of the "individual pinch of destiny" that is ours alone. The self is neither a thing nor a thought, but a meaningful life that includes desiring, hoping, believing, willing, sorrowing, rejoicing, sharing, and indeed all of the intentional experiences that make up our odyssey in the world.

In claiming that the self is not to be thought of as "all there" or as a prior essence that merely unfolds in time, but rather as a centered life-in-the-making through freedom, one need not be saying that the self is an entirely subsequent or future affair. In the first place, to regard the self as a task and an achievement is also to recognize that the individual whose task it is already has the necessary human endowments for carrying out the task. There must be present a self of an incipient sort as the precondition of becoming a fully developed self. This paradox cannot be avoided simply by envisaging the self as wholly constituted by the adoption in the present of some project. For even to project a plan presupposes a self-conscious being capable of envisaging it and of finding it sufficiently valuable to be pursued. In the end, what paradox there may be belongs to the nature of becoming itself. That there is a real and definite process of becoming means that some end or objective is not yet, that it is lacking in the cross-section of the present but is a real possibility for the future. That lack, however, that absence leaving room for further development, does not exhaust the situation or reduce it to a mere nothing. What is to become, in this case the mature and centered self, is still related to the present and actual self striving to work out its own destiny. The chief reason why we fail to understand real becoming, as Whitehead and others have pointed out, is that we overlook the presence of *tendency* or directionality manifesting itself in all growth and creativity. Classical empiricism had no place for tendency in the course of experience and events because it was unable to find an impression corresponding to it. That, however, must be regarded as a shortcoming of the old empiricism and the belief that the ultimate constituents of experience must be clear-cut and atomic data that are in themselves static. Tendency *ipso facto* cannot be such a datum and it was ignored. It is, however, very much an ingredient in all process and helps to explain how something comes to be, not out of nothing, but from an actuality pregnant with real possibilities.

A second reason why the self cannot be construed entirely in futuristic terms is that it must be present as a whole with unity and coherence at every stage of the process of development. It cannot make its appearance only at the end of the temporal route. In this sense the self, like consciousness, is always present in every attempt to show either how it comes about or how it supposedly can be replaced by something else. We see this in James's bold declaration that consciousness does not exist and his attempt to account for the functions previously assigned to it. His strategy was to return to the stream of experience with its bits of pure experience and then to claim for these items some remarkable capacities. My bits are, in his view, "warmer" to me than yours are to me, and vice-versa. My bits "recognize" each other as forming part of the same stream of awareness. In short, these pure experiences can perform the necessary functions only because they have already been endowed with consciousness, so that, far from disappearing, consciousness seems to have multiplied instead. James's proposal to do away with "con-sciousness" and try to get along with what he called "sciousness"— a kind of awareness not focused or presided over by a unifying center of intention represented by the "con" in "consciousness"— is parallel to an effort to dispense with the self by distributing the power to direct the course of the individual's experience over the particular items of experience as if they had some special capacity to unify and organize themselves.

We need to avoid the pitfalls noted at the outset which serve to obscure the relations between an agent and its conduct. For, as we saw earlier, there is no point in trying to understand freedom as self-determination if we continue to view the relation between the self and its actions as a relation either between objects or between isolated acts and a collection of experiences lacking any unifying center. The self is neither a substance nor a collection of episodes of experience brought together under the rubric of memory; it is instead a meaningful, temporal biography unified by a dominant purpose expressing what the person means to be and to become, a purpose that allows for the identity and persistence of the individual over time and change so far as he or she continues to remain faithful to and reaffirm that purpose as the basis of self-determination.

Self-determination is what James would have called a "double-barrelled" affair. On the one hand, there is the determining and partial making of the self in particular deeds and in unified courses of action intended to carry out particular plans or purposes. On the other hand, we encounter the more comprehensive task of determining the self as a whole through discovery of and commitment to the dominant purpose that defines what we mean to be.

The latter we shall call the formation of a character, a certain permanency and consistency in the values we acknowledge and the ways we behave, to which we freely commit ourselves and which we seek to realize in our daily life. The two sides of self-determination develop together, since it is our enduring self that we are seeking to realize in all of our particular actions. That enduring self, though partially determined by factors beyond ourselves, is the self we are trying to discover and remain faithful to in the course of our actions and experiences. Hence when we speak of self-determination as the mark of freedom, we must understand the effort ingredient in actual willing as embracing the determining of the self in specific actions and courses of action as well as the whole and enduring self represented by what I have called having a character.

In order to grasp this formula for freedom more precisely, we must consider what we mean by will and by character. To begin with, of all the so-called faculties claimed for human beings, will is best suited for being understood in terms of *willing;* in grammatical terms, the participle is closer to what actually happens than is the noun. The question is, what are the ingredients in what we may call the "activity situation," and how are they related to each other? Largely due to the prevalence of the common-sense division of our capacities into affective, cognitive, and voluntary, the latter has come to be identified with effort and efficacy exclusively, so that much of what is contained in actual willing is left out of account. It is the whole self or person who acts and not some separate entity called the "will," and hence we must expect that in willing all of our powers will be involved. I propose to delineate some four features that enter into the activity situation as we experience it in all that we do. These are: preference, purpose, power, and perseverance.

Preference points to our capacity to evaluate both goals and the actions needed to realize them. By preference I do not mean whims, caprices, and that sort of thing, so much in evidence at present, expressed by the phrase, "I feel that . . ." without further justification. Preference means a self-conscious choice made in accordance with an acknowledged norm, implying that what is chosen is good or right in that case as over against other alternatives. The acknowledged norm, moreover, indicates the value or values to which the person seeks to remain loyal in determining himself or herself, in both the choice and the subsequent action. In this sense, the self is "under orders," that is, self-imposed orders to be faithful to the norm that helps to define the self we mean to be. And, as we shall see, failure to sustain that faithfulness leads to the self's becoming alien to itself, not to the extent of becoming somebody else, but in the consciousness that we have acted out of character and have not realized the self we meant to be.

All willing requires purpose, since it is a venture into the future and as human conduct must be guided through what is often a maze of possibilities and alternatives. The presence of purpose distinguishes human action from mere movement and involuntary response. Purpose as intention or an "end in view" expresses what we mean to do on particular occasions and what we mean to be on all occasions. Willing as self-determination embraces both particular purposes and the overarching purpose or plan that unifies, defines, and identifies us as that individual and no other. Thus we have self-determination in realizing the purpose in the act and the more comprehensive determination of the self in helping to bring about the self of the overarching purpose to which we strive to remain loyal.

The third ingredient in willing is power, or the actual effort we are able to muster for the accomplishment of the deed. We are directly aware of this power through our sense of willing in the making, a sense that comes to the fore by way of living through opposition and struggle. In physical situations — pushing a table across the room, opening a door that refuses to yield, sifting through a clay mound in search of a lost artifact — we have a direct awareness of the effort we are expending against what opposes us and exerts its own obstructing force in the opposite direction. The strength of our effort in these situations is indeterminate in the double sense that (1) our power may be inadequate to overcome the obstacle even when accompanied by the greatest resolve, and (2) our resolve may weaken so that our effort is lessened and we fail, even though we might have succeeded if we had persevered. The point is that the power we actually have in given situations is an indeterminate mixture of resolve and effort, on the one hand, and the force of the circumstances, on the other. In moral situations our awareness of power is no less evident to us than in the foregoing instances. The sense of power to decide and execute the act is never more vivid than in situations where we have a conviction about what we should do if we are to remain loyal to the moral norm that defines us and yet at the same time find ourselves rebelling against the very thought of going through with the deed. It goes against what we want to do, against our sense of pride at the prospect of humiliation, and against any number of other factors that would lead us to succumb and fail to make the effort in the proper direction. Even when we fail we still have the lingering sense that we could have put forth the effort needed to succeed. So the idea of self-determination remains, and the best that we can do in such situations is to say to ourselves that we were not self-determined enough. Failure to produce the deed or the project, however, is not an indication of the lack of freedom, because only a being with freedom could fail. In the absence of freedom there would be neither success nor failure but only the occurrence of the one deed that had to happen regardless of the nature of the individual self to whom it is attributed. There is, curiously enough, a moral sense in which something "had to happen" in the way of human action, and this will appear later on in connection with the idea of self-determination as the persistent willing of a person's character.

The last characteristic of willing, perseverance, does in fact lead directly into a consideration of the capacity of the self to forge and sustain a character which is the most distinctive feature of the freedom of the human person. This characteristic, like the others, has two faces. One points in the direction of actions and courses of action, and the other in the direction not of action so much as of being. We often speak, and rightly, of a person who is determined to carry out a project to the limit of his or her ability. By this we mean that that individual is willing to persevere, not to be distracted or diverted, but to continue to pursue the project until it is completed. Such determination or persistence is necessary for a course of action involving a series of events that can be brought to a conclusion only if the individual continues to sustain the resolve over time and in the face of hazards and trials. This virtue expresses the capacity of the self to remain loyal, as Royce put it, to causes whose realization is like the city out of sight. We work in the hope that our effort will not be in vain, although we may often have little immediate sense that the cause is being advanced or that what we do in its behalf makes any appreciable difference. The extended causes of social and political responsibility—the struggle for peace, the fight for a more just society, the effort to overcome the ills of humanity, from the plight of the homeless at home, to the misery of the hungry both at home and abroad—demand people of perseverance who can find the resources to remain devoted to such causes as far transcend those more visible and tangible projects whose progress may be more a matter of sight than of faith and hope.

Perseverance shows itself in the deeper dimension of the self's loyalty to its own overarching and defining purpose. Spinoza spoke of persevering in one's being, which he identified as the *conatus*, or that combination of will and desire motivated by the intellectual love of God sustaining us in our journey toward a goal we do not see. In our terms, this means the effort to realize our freedom in a continuing loyalty and commitment to that self we mean to be—that self which is in the making through all the deeds we have performed in accordance with the values we acknowledge and regard as the being of ourselves. Perseverance leads to the formation of a character, that sustained complex quality in our temporal biography that identifies us and constitutes our integrity. Kant made an important contribution when he proposed the distinction between having a nature and developing a character. Objects have natures in the form of a set of qualities and powers manifesting themselves consistently under specific circumstances and enabling us to identify them by knowing what they would be like or how they would behave if they are objects of a certain kind. Character is to a person as nature is to an object, but with a crucial difference. Objects may be regarded as having their natures through a cosmic order, whereas character is an ethical achievement through freedom. Even if it becomes what we may call a "second nature," as shown by consistency in behavior, character is never an automatic affair, because we must continue to will to be that kind of person or to be loyal to that character. To regard a person as someone of honesty and responsibility, for instance, is to come to expect those traits to continue to show themselves in the conduct of that person. There is, however, no guarantee that this will happen, precisely because the element of freedom remains.

The person of responsibility and honesty may fail to remain loyal to that character, either temporarily or in some more permanent vein, and for myriad reasons. This failure we deplore. On the other side of the ledger we must take account of the possibility, again in freedom, of the development of an evil character. Consider someone who has no hesitation in treating persons as things or who scoffs at social responsibility and regards morality as a sham or a device invented by the weak to corrupt the strong. It is important to notice that in this case, too, that evil character persists as long as the individual continues to will to be that kind of person. The doctrine of self-determination allows, however, for the possibility of a transformation and, paradoxically enough, that can happen only if the person should fail to persist in those evil ways and become reoriented. This failure we applaud. Freedom, then, is no guarantee for the righteous and no comfort for the wicked, since our conception of the self as in the making means that it is never finally fixed but allows for change and development in both moral directions.

I wish now to offer three illustrations from the lives of Socrates, Antigone, and Martin Luther. Each of these cases, despite their widely different circumstances, exhibits essentially the same sort of personal and moral dilemma, or "crisis," understood in its original sense as an event in which we are judged. In each, some concrete action is called for in a situation where the character of the individual is put to the test and in such a way as to involve a supreme reaffirmation of the self as a whole, the self that defines the being of the person.

Socrates was brought to trial in ancient Athens, charged with corrupting the young and failing to pay due respect to the traditional deities. As for leading the young astray, Socrates did no more than attempt, as the gadfly, to drive them to think for themselves and to get at the truth about the soul. As for the deities, it is most likely that the Athenians, insofar as they understood Socrates' teaching at all, supposed that those "ideas" or "forms," ideas of the good, of courage, of knowledge, and of the soul, were something of the sort of new deities to replace the old. Socrates was condemned and ordered to drink the poison hemlock. Socrates believed that he had been judged unfairly. Yet he was finally not persuaded to make his escape unlawfully, because he had long maintained that the laws nourish us and are just, despite human injustice. Were he to escape illegally in that situation he would in effect be giving the lie to his entire life. The character he fashioned, the self to which he was determined to remain loyal, would be totally contradicted and set at nought. Socrates could have done other than he did in this final decision, and he was under a great deal of pressure to change his mind. But if he had done so, he would no longer have been Socrates, and that is the crux of the matter. To be and continue to be Socrates, he had to do what he did. This is self-determination in the ultimate sense.

We know Antigone, the ancient Greek heroine and daughter of Oedipus, most vividly in the play of Sophocles where her story is told. To begin with, her loyalty was first displayed when she accompanied her father in his exile and disgrace and helped to lighten the onus of that humiliation. Her most agonizing test was yet to come. Both of her brothers, Eteocles and Polynices, were killed in the war known to classicists and ancient historians as "The Seven against Thebes" and directed against the Satrap of the land, Creon. He had ruled that Polynices, whose body often appears in dramatic productions lying uncovered on a strip of sand, should have no burial. Antigone, true to her own sacred tradition, could not accept this decree. She was faced with the conflict between the law she acknowledged and the command of an alien lord. She had to choose between the desecration of her brother and obedience to the power of a tyrant. Her decision was made in accordance with her character. She performed the forbidden burial rites over her brother and was made to pay the price of being buried herself, alive in a cave, as the tradition has it. It is clear that Antigone could have done otherwise, but, as in the case of Socrates, to have done so would have resulted in her ceasing to be Antigone, that self she meant to be. For to be Antigone was to be the person who could only remain loyal to the character she had developed.

The most decisive event in the life of Martin Luther, after the posting in 1517 of the famous theses, was his appearance at the Diet of Worms three years later, at which the emperor at the command of the pope was to carry out officially the Bull of Excommunication issued after Luther's debates with Eck. In those exchanges, Luther was forced to make clear his departure from a number of Roman Catholic doctrines expressed in such a writing as "The Freedom of a Christian." It was the hope of the papal authorities that Luther would recant and admit his errors as a prelude to reconciliation. Of course, he did not; and his ringing statement reinforcing his views—"Here I stand; I can do no other" —still echoes in the annals of freedom, loyalty, and courage. Of the three cases noted, this is perhaps the most pointed because of the specific language uttered. "I can do no other" is the paradigm of self-determination. As with Socrates and Antigone, of course, he could have done other. He could have refused to attend the Diet in the first instance, and he could have retracted his convictions. That freedom of possibility was certainly something of which he was aware, especially in view of the fact that his life was in danger, but he had a higher loyalty. Had he done otherwise, he would have ceased to be Martin Luther by being disloyal to that self which defined him as that character and no other.

In the end, the important lesson taught by the idea of freedom as self-determination is an austere one. Everything depends upon the quality and character of the self that is to do the determining. If the unexamined life is, as Socrates taught, not worth living, perhaps we should consider whether a self without character is worth determining.

6
Freedom and the State
FRITHJOF BERGMANN

I

THE MOST GOVERNING METAPHOR for our American idea of freedom is the picture of unfetteredness. The opposite of freedom is therefore for us the obstructed, the manacled, and the locked in. The quintessence of the unfree person is the one behind bars. The incarnation of the free person is the roaming cowboy of the plains.

This idea, which is nothing less than the lighthouse beacon of our culture, needs circumspection and much care. For if by freedom we mean the absence of obstacles, it certainly cannot be achieved, and it is therefore not something that can be offered to someone, either by an individual, an institution, or a government. No relationship to any other person—be it child or parent, lover, friend, or traveling companion—is without hindrances, obstacles, and little obligations at every twist and turn. Even during a breakfast conversation, my now talking limits the start of your next sentence; the piece of toast I take is out of your grasp and you are forced to take another. If one seriously attempted to eliminate all obstacles, the effort would be a dizzying inconsequential flurry. The actual accomplishment of it is absurdly and hopelessly out of the question. One should ask whether even an interesting fantasy of such a society, not just without rules, but "without any fences"—one that would allow everyone to roam unobstructed in every conceivable three-dimensional direction—is imaginable. Nothing could approach it! Age, gravity, even indigestion would have to be suspended!

So, the idea of freedom that is most persuasive and deeply rooted in our culture promises a vision that is hopelessly out of reach. A condition of genuine unhinderedness could be realized only in a setting of total and black emptiness. To move in the direction where one could offer someone a world in which the sum of all obstacles had been removed would actually end with a world that would be emptier and thinner. It would be a world in which one would tumble like an unmoored, ricocheting traveler in space. To say that it would have to be a world of solitude and isolation is still to use nostalgic, velvet-covered words. The crude fact is that one could not survive. The prize of doing away with all obstacles would be a literal crib death.

So to reach this idea of freedom in its full extremity would be a dreadful calamity. But matters are still worse. It is not only appalling when we push it to its logical — and therefore possibly absurd — extreme, but the flaws make themselves felt even when we approach it by degrees.

Take a typical family situation: Many parents have come to doubt the inherited, staid values and have therefore decided to give their children at least one gift, namely "freedom." We all know the story. These parents often make a great effort not to put obstacles in their children's way, and that means moving back and renouncing ever larger areas of space. This can continue until the parents live spread-eagled flat against the walls. Unsurprisingly, pandemonium breaks loose and grows until it reigns in all parts of the house. The structure of common meals collapses. Dirty dishes pile up in precariously balanced towers. Orange marmalade glues the piano keys together into a single solid slab. Then, at last, pushed beyond the limits of their stretched endurance, these parents come crashing down from their high perches and stride through the rooms shouting threats of imminent recrimination. Predictably enough, such parents feel crestfallen soon after, and this starts the next turn of the cycle. Appalled, they flee away from what they have just done, press themselves now still more self-effacingly against the walls, and cling there even longer. Yet ineluctably, sooner or later their staying power is once more overtaxed, and this time they come crashing down with still more inflamed vituperation.

This downward spiral is an endemic consequence of this idea

of freedom, and the end result to which it leads constitutes the third and most serious danger of this idea of freedom. This is the exhaustion and cynicism, the eventual paralysis and even nihilism that this idea engenders. How could it be otherwise? The back-and-forth of the alternation would be stupefying by itself, but there is in addition the utterly disorienting sense that one progresses into an ever more unsupportable and ghoulish condition, precisely whenever one comes closer to the goals for which one strives. How could one not come to scorn the entire puppet show of values? And this corresponds to the facts. After enough arm wrestling, a vast number of parents now tap their way along a safe middle-of-the-road, without a shred of genuine conviction. They have heard enough from enough quacks of all persuasions and they no longer want to think. They have joined the enormous funeral procession assembled for what Hegel called the death of thought.

Exactly the same pattern, inscribed by the same systemic logic, is sadly familiar to us from a context larger than that of the family. We have also witnessed the same back-and-forth motion in the educational establishment. Could it have been more graphic than in the last wide swing? First it swung away from all structure, from even the most minimal organization, during the late sixties, which gave us the opportunity to see, with special vividness, just how destructive and debilitating the pursuit of this idea of freedom can become. Any interference or influence from teachers was understood to be an imposition or a violation of autonomy, and teachers, like parents, moved themselves out of the way, until all teaching was proscribed and only a slow tumbling and turning in empty space remained. Was anyone surprised by the reaction? How could there not have been a frenetic rushing back to the opposite extreme — back to discipline, back to authority, and back to basics? Possibly we are now close to yet another swing of the pendulum, for one could easily trace back the same dementing tick-tock all the way to the beginning of modern educational theory, in Pestalozzi, Herder, and Rousseau. This explains how whole regions of the educational system fell into the same condition of cynical indifference and contemptuous paralysis in which so many parents find themselves.

II

With this brief summary of the basics of "obstacle thinking" behind us, we turn to the pivotal notion that "the government which governs best is the government which governs least." We need to distance ourselves from that dictum and ask: Whatever gave it the semblance of self-evidence? On the face of it one would not say this of a teacher, or a doctor, or a parent—that the teacher who teaches least, or the doctor who barely ever cures, or the parent who does least for the children, is on that account the best! Why, if not with these others, should this minimalism nonetheless be appropriate for the state?

This statement only becomes obviously true if one forgets the basics which we just rehearsed. If one focuses on the question of what bestows upon this proposition its air of self-evidence, then one answer is that this happens if one slips into the fantasy that the state is the *only* source of obstacles which limit us. That delusion makes it natural to imagine that less state means more freedom, and that less state is therefore patently superior.

A comparison to the confusions surrounding the discussions of academic freedom might help to explain further what I mean. If one keeps in mind that all decisions which researchers make are naturally, inevitably, and rightly subject to myriad pressures—having to do with what is fashionable, acceptable to prestigious journals, benevolently viewed by foundations, and so forth—then one is not apt to feel that one additional restriction, say, a restriction on doing research directly related to the destruction of human beings, is tantamount to ending academic freedom. If one is aware of the elementary logic of "obstacle thinking" we just sketched, then one knows that this discussion would have to be far more complex. Questions about how different obstacles relate to each other, whether decreasing one will have the effect of increasing others, and the like, would have to be raised. So the obviousness is no longer there, and it is the seeming patency of this celebrated dictum that is of main concern to us. If, on the other hand, one allows oneself to slip into the fantasy that the pursuit of truth is somehow entirely pristine and "free" (that is, not sullied by pressures from a spate of mundane forces), then the appearance is created that suddenly and with one blow the previously pure condition has been defiled, and that with this one incursion academic freedom was eclipsed.

Some people's thinking about government runs on parallel tracks. If we imagine that no other obstacles exist, and forget that having obstacles might be positively good, then the notion that less government would automatically mean fewer obstacles, and that this would therefore be instantly equivalent to greater freedom, is able to spring up. This may seem offensively unintelligent, but what else would make it evident and plain that greater freedom is the other side of smaller government?

Even if one only acknowledged that, of course, any number of other forces represent hindrances — that debilities, hunger, ignorance, and lack of work limit us just as effectively as ordinances, or the police — the issue begins to be more complex. And needless to say, this is still doltish and clay-footed thinking, since some obstacles the government establishes might be obstacles only for a small number, and on balance these might increase the sum of freedom since the hindrances imposed on some will reduce the limitations for a far greater number. In addition, all obstacles are certainly not made of the same stuff, and it is therefore not like adding up so many apples. Again another set of doors is opened once one grants that the reduction of obstacles is not the only goal at stake, but that other values — most obviously peace, security, and comfort — should also figure in the calculation. Once that has been admitted the trade-offs easily reveal that more government could on several counts create more freedom — and could also in other ways be "better."

It is critical to grasp that more government can mean more freedom, and that this is so not in some elusive or slippery or double-bottomed Hegelian sense, but in one that is very graspable and firm. Nothing is easier than to say that outside of the state we have greater "license" but that "genuine freedom" requires social institutions which include the state. But this is only a highbrow version of name calling. Just what the deficient qualities in "license" are and how exactly it is different from "genuine freedom" remains opaque — and the upshot is therefore only an intimidated silence. The advantage of the straightforward thinking which the concept of obstacles allows is that the intended meaning becomes very clear.

We should recognize that, especially in the United States, a powerful cultural and psychological predisposition toward thinking of the state as unavoidably curtailing freedom is endemic. There is a strong impulse to accept that freedom must of course be limited in some measure by the state, but that this limitation should be no more than is indispensably required. Psychologically the opposite tradition, which in important ways derives from Hegel, where the state *increases* freedom, has never gained a foothold in this country. Yet my hope is that rethinking matters in the plain terminology of obstacles might open some hitherto closed minds.

Some examples of possible calculations run like this:

1. A state can impose limitations on everyone, but on balance these reduce for everyone the sum total of obstacles they face, and the result is thus greater freedom in that straightforward sense. This could be illustrated even in very homely ways: Think of traffic regulations and the thousands of other regulations that are structurally like them. It is a fact that I am, of course, limited by rules, but on balance I can still drive vastly faster and to many more places than I could if neither I nor anyone else were "restricted" by these rules.

2. The state can impose limitations that will affect only a very few, where the limitations on these few may not be very personal and in addition may pertain only to one narrow sphere in which these citizens only occasionally act. The state may do this not just for the greater security and comfort, but for the greater freedom, of a very much larger number. Here too one could choose from a cornucopia of examples, but restrictions on certain business transactions, like hostile takeovers, or mergers, or plant closings, are all cases in point.

3. Americans are prone to a kind of schizophrenic thinking. On the one hand, some of the most evocative and guiding dicta of our history elevate the government of this country, not just above other governments, but also above other far less savory social forces. That government should be of, by, and for the people is an idea that rightly has been nailed into the landscape of this country with railroad spikes. But how does that conviction combine with

the prejudice against the state? If we remember the basics about obstacles, then it seems inescapable that limiting the government will often mean that other forces—which may not be of, and for, and by the people, but will be clandestine forces which work darkly, behind closed doors and under carpets—fill the vacuum. These will then make the obstacles which I and others face much greater and far more debilitating.

The government represents one of many agencies in the context that is our social life and is the one force that is relatively open and relatively accountable to us, while over numerous others we have no control at all. Thus it seems bizarre that we should be so afraid of this one obviously far from perfect, but at least not hopeless, force. Many of the most painful aspects associated with the Third World result from weak governments that try to function in an environment of very powerful "secret societies" or "gangs," which operate in many ways like organized crime. And if the choice is between government and business, then it is very much an open question. It depends on how open and accessible a government in fact is, but also on how close to the spirit and the operation of organized crime certain corporations are.

We can now follow up with a different approach. Another way of responding to the notion that minimal government is obviously better would be to ask: Why not be consistent? If the less the better, then clearly doing away with government completely would be best of all.

It is safe to say that many who call fire and brimstone down on government are not really prepared for a full-scale flesh-and-blood establishment of anarchism. In fact, many who call themselves anarchists ignore some of the considerations we adduced, in particular the idea that getting rid of the state of course does not mean that one is rid of all who would yield authority. On the contrary, the situations are legion where the elimination of a dubious but in some ways "legitimate" authority opens the door to rednecks and goons and all the different colors of brown-shirts. If one bore this in mind, then much of the facile deprecation of the state could be seen as just one other symptom of the deeply ingrained prejudice against the state. What is more, one could ask whether Marx's wish for the "withering away of the state" is not yet another symptom of this dubious predisposition.

This refusal to go forward to the conclusion which the "least is best" dictum implies leads to one cardinal consideration. Many who flamboyantly declare "the less government the better" do not say *what they actually mean.* Their hesitancy to embrace anarchism is one tell-tale symptom of this fact. But a closer look will tell us more.

III

This paper is meant to throw a beam of light on a phenomenon that seems to me grotesque. It is an instance of a weird upside-down inversion which could not possibly occur in nature, but only in the bewitched world of ideological inventions. I refer to the astounding linkage of the rhetoric of freedom with conservatism in America. Integral to the strangeness of this phenomenon is that it presents itself as a matter of course, and this not least through sheer reiteration. It has now become a seemingly predestined liaison. We have all come to acknowledge that conservatives are skeptical of government and Washington, and that they hate federal meddling. Being for freedom seems to many not even the other side of the same coin, but the identical same thing. And the spectacle of our recent history which conservatives project for us has a neatly corresponding plot. Under the aegis of liberalism the lush growing vines of government were allowed to curl and spread unchecked, until their growth had all of us in Gulliver-like fetters. That was the cue for conservatives to come to our rescue, and ever since they have pruned and clipped and chopped away at this oppressive foliage, to give us new vigor and fresh air.

To my mind even the words *conservative* and *free* do not couple, so a first question is: How was it possible that this marriage was arranged and that it came to be perceived as made in heaven? I believe that the answer to this question has much to do with the gap between what is said and what is meant.

One immediate indication of the width of this crevasse becomes apparent when the very same voices who insist that government must be pushed back, as if it were a mudslide, call also for "law and order." These two are the most direct opposites. On one side one hoists up pronouncements that "government should be kept out of all aspects of our lives," but a moment later one wants government to enter not only the privacy of our homes but be allowed into the bedroom to there "regulate" who is allowed to enter whom.

Again, the very same chorus that cannot say enough about the strangling hands of government, which supposedly kill all enterprise and spirit and initiative, *want* these same paws in the world of art, where spirit, compared to the world of business, is apt to be more present and more volatile. Not in the airlines, but in museums, libraries, and movie houses do they want government regulation — and preferably in uniform and armed.

Or again, the very same group that one moment insists that the green grass of prosperity cannot ever grow where the foot of government has trodden, will one breath later blow down a whole wall of protections, painstakingly designed to limit and control the government. When it is a matter of the precise rights of the accused, or the exact procedures under which police are allowed to question, or the difficult rules under which damaging evidence can be admitted — all these ways of putting the government behind fences — they would just as soon tear down. But when the government puts some conditions on the gases that cars can emit, then this seems to happen on the other side of a thick wall.

It would be easy to add a long string of examples. It is more useful, however, to recognize that we are not dealing with an even split, where the state in some situations is invited in but is also in just as many pushed back and rejected. With many of the most audible conservatives the situation is far more extreme. It is only one small area from which many of them would drive government, principally the area of business transactions, mergers, takeovers, and the like — and of course also the area of the so-called protections, be it of minorities, or of disadvantaged people, or of the environment. Into virtually all other rooms and spaces these conservatives do not just allow the state; they want to ensconce it on a platform with nightstick and handgun and the use of the electric chair.

The often invoked division between the political and the economic sphere — that conservatives want economic freedom and liberals political freedom — does not apply. For even inside the economic segment strange partitions are obeyed. If a bill has not been paid — surely an economic matter — then the full force of the governmental penal system is invoked, and the talk about "living our lives without governmental interference" turns into an embarrassed clearing of one's throat. Or, conversely, the sanctified doctrines of the free market suddenly lose all their force if it is prostitutes who want to expand their business enterprise.

The heart of conservatism, not just politically, but as a general cultural stance, is a very high resistance to deviations, or, bluntly, to anything perceived as "different." There is no evidence, for example, that the conservative way of dressing is more intelligent, or healthy, or aesthetically pleasing than some other ways, but it is the way in which *one* dresses — and woe and ridicule and ostracism for those who swerve. It extends backward into one's pedigree, and from there even into the cavity of one's own mouth — for the shape one gives to one's vowels counts — and of course from there in all directions, to the way in which the "right," tone-setting people hold a fork, or marry, or play golf.

Not just in relation to the state, but in regard to virtually all other of life's circumstances conservatism defends barriers, and yet it claims to have rung the bell of freedom. True, some conservatives will concede that freedom is a grand, but treacherous and abused, word; and they will then assert that what really irks them is the sheer maddening inefficiency and the profligate and sickening wastefulness of big government. But how could any reasonable person possibly disagree with that? Of course some government undertakings are miserably ineffectual and, worse, criminal and corrupt. It is wrong, however, to imagine that this is inherent in the deep-seated nature of government, or that it is endemic to the state. Even the flightiest international comparison should be enough to dispel that presumption. Anyone who has ever experienced the awesome punctuality of the *Deutsche Bahn* — very much government-owned and run — and has compared it to any aspect of an American privately owned airline would see that the differences can count the other way. And in case one supposes that the Prussian tradition is responsible for this, one could go to Mexico and there notice that the nationalized Pemex Petroleum refineries have immaculately maintained grounds and a perpetually brand-new black and orange coat of paint. Surely this is not an idiosyncrasy of foreign countries. There are impressive examples here at home.

Moreover, have we not read enough all-too-human stories

about the pratfalls of privately owned American corporations? And is one not forced to conclude from the general desperateness of American business, and its buckling helplessness the very first time it encounters genuine competition, that these are not isolated anecdotes but that they are representative of a prevailing pattern? Would there be a new crop of bestsellers every month about the "pursuit of excellence" if excellence did not seem very rare and mostly far away?

With all this one could wonder why we have just at this juncture an adulation of the business ethos, and a cult of the executive —with executive suites, homes, limousines, airport lounges, and the rest? Why now, at the very point at which sharp disappointment and anger would seem much more justified? If a football team got beaten as consistently as American corporations have, the fans would grow cold and stay away. Why are we so indulgent with the failure of so many privately owned enterprises that cost us so much more?

Where has this discussion led us in regard to freedom? The usurpation of the rhetoric of freedom by American conservatism is breathtaking and fantastic. In Europe that usurpation would be unthinkable. That conservatism is tied to nationalism, militarism, and inherited wealth is there so obvious that this disguise would never work. Conservatives are *not* consistently or across a significantly broad spectrum "against government," or even in favor of a more contained and bridled use of it.

I stress the two levels of the picture I have tried to paint. On one of these levels the conservative claim to the rhetoric of freedom has been countered directly. But this is only one plateau. We should not slip back into even-handed equanimity and say again that liberalism emphasizes political freedom while conservatism stresses the freedom of the economic. Much could be said about whether they are really halves, or whether liberals have not sought to reduce a great variety of different obstacles and, importantly, obstacles that impede the desires of the great majority, while conservatism has defended oddly shaped and not even very satisfying privileges of a very few. But this discussion would still be on the same preliminary level. The deeper and philosophically more strenuous and ambitious considerations take us back to the beginning of this paper.

An underlying realization should have crystallized, namely, that in any talk of obstacles we must be very much on our guard. The apparent gentlemen's agreement, to which we just alluded, is just another instance of the traps to which it leads, or of one more bout of arm wrestling that is bound to produce exhaustion and paralysis. We should understand that the boast that "less state creates more freedom" is wildly questionable even if it were meant. As we saw, it raises further questions about what in place of the state will fill the vacuum, about whether these other forces are perhaps much worse than the state we now have, and, beyond this, whether the built-in presupposition that more state always means less freedom is not absurd.

7
Science, Theology, and Freedom: A New Look at the Galileo Case
JAMES R. LANGFORD

THE CONDEMNATION OF GALILEO by the Holy Office in 1633 is one of the most written-about events in history. Polemicists, apologists, historians, playwrights, and novelists have produced literally thousands of books, essays, and significant articles about Galileo, his life, work, and legacy.

For some, notably John W. Draper and Andrew Dickson White, Galileo was the symbol of the trail-blazing, truth-bearing scientist hounded by theologians bent on orthodoxy at any cost, even that of human life. In Draper's *History of the Conflict between Religion and Science* (1874) and White's book *A History of the Warfare of Science with Theology in Christendom* (1896), Galileo and science versus religion (mainly the Catholic Church) was the centerpiece of the conflict-and-warfare thesis.

These and similar anti-Catholic polemics brought out Catholic apologists in force. Attempts were made to assert that it was Christian theology and medieval Catholic thought that made possible the entire scientific enterprise in the first place. Other defenders of the faith soft-pedalled documents or split hairs in inventing new and less severe definitions of the word *heretical*. Finally, some took pleasure in pointing out that Luther, Calvin, and Melanchthon had been anti-Copernican too.

In the 1950s several major works appeared with Galileo as the focus. Bertold Brecht's play *The Life of Galileo* dramatized the Galileo symbol but with a difference. Brecht's Galileo is a man without courage as he recants the truth to save his life. Georgio de Santillana's powerful recitation of the story almost canonizes Galileo at the expense of a corrupt and unscrupulous cadre within the circles of power in Rome. And arguing to the contrary there was the anti-Galileo version of Arthur Koestler in *The Sleepwalkers*, an immensely popular and well-written work, notable in its advocacy of the need to suppress daydreaming scientists in Galileo's time—or in ours.

Subsequent works by historians of science and historians of theology have in recent years achieved a much greater understanding of the complexity of the case and consequently a more balanced presentation of it. Excellent scholarly studies have now detailed Galileo's educational background and sources, the gradual development of Copernicanism, and a much deeper appreciation of the many trends and countertrends that influenced the characters and outcome of the drama.

Recently, a whole spate of articles and reviews has been prompted by the publication of Pietro Redondi's *Galileo: Heretic*, which claims that atomism, not astronomy, was what lay behind the infamous condemnation of Galileo.[1]

Aside from providing Galileo scholars with occasional employment giving talks or writing reviews, the seemingly endless interest in his saga indicates that although scholars probably have found and identified all of the pieces of the puzzle, no one has yet put it together in such a way that once and for all the whole story can be told in a definitive version.

It is interesting to note that in trying to reconstruct the lines and patterns, facts and nuances of the story, we face the same epistemological hurdle that befuddled the scientific, theological, and philosophical competitors more than 350 years ago—the question of certitude. We have historical facts and documents, contemporary correspondence, the complete dossier from the archives of the Holy Office. We now know a great deal about even the minor characters in the story and we know enough to be aware that simplified causal explanations do not suffice; chance and circumstance played more than bit parts in the drama as well.

Still, it may be that with all of our knowledge the best we can do is to piece together a facsimile of what happened—not perfect, but good enough to let us see clearly what the moral of the story might be. We are looking for more than slogans or grand gestures; we are in search of some wisdom of the kind that will help us recognize the issues should they surface in new garb in our time. That wisdom might also help us cope with their complexity rather than to seek solutions in simplicity.

Let us begin with what happened, staying as much as possible within the realm of fact. Then we can try to understand why it happened and whether it might have been avoided. Finally, let us hear the echoes of Galileo and his opponents to see whether the aftermath might also serve as a forewarning.

Galileo was born on February 15, 1564, at Pisa, Italy. The world into which he was born was alive with postmedieval ferment, including the discovery of new worlds and the opening of new trade routes, the forging of new political alliances and the expansion of educational opportunity. But it was three movements —the Reformation, the Counter-Reformation, and the Renaissance —that made the most critical impact on what has been rightly called the "Age of Adventure."

The Reformation was not a sudden mass defection begun when Martin Luther posted his ninety-five theses on the church door in 1517. Abuses in the church had been rampant for some time; a poorly trained and often undisciplined clergy, the sterility of a scholastic intellectualism which had detached theology from its biblical roots, and a papacy that had lost much of its former political and spiritual authority all made reform a necessity.

Declaring independence from Rome, the Protestant Reformers challenged the church's teaching on free will, grace, the sacraments, and papal prerogatives. Within twenty years, northern Germany and Scandinavia had become Lutheran, Switzerland and part of France were Calvinist, and England had a national church. Hatred, persecution, and wars of religion were to plague the continent well into the next century.

The reform movement away from Rome brought on a Counter-Reformation within the Catholic Church. In 1545 an ecumenical council convened at Trent in Italy, and over the next eighteen years the Council of Trent defined the church's position on doctrines— particularly those challenged by Protestants—and laid down strict disciplinary measures as part of a strong program of reform. Naturally, Trent was a call back to tradition; it was careful, conservative, and precise, perhaps rigid, in its formulation of beliefs, using mainly the vocabulary of Aristotelian-Thomist philosophy and theology. The Council of Trent ended the year before Galileo was born, but its jealous passion for orthodoxy, particularly in the area of scriptural interpretation, was to play a crucial role in the story of his life.

The third important movement of the time was the Renaissance, which revived the classic texts and styles of the ancients, both pagan and Christian. The texts renewed interest in questions such as the power of nature and human dignity; and that interest led on the one hand to the close study of classic positions such as those of Plato and Aristotle, and on the other hand to the imaginative thinking of Pico, Nicholas of Cusa, Ficino, Paracelsus, Cardano, Telesio, Campanella, Persio, Bruno, and others — especially of the Neoplatonist bent — who fostered antiauthoritarian, anti-Aristotelian, and decidedly novel views of nature and the human condition. But the notion that modern science was born in a sudden outburst of empirical, rational rebellion against everything Aristotelian is pure myth. Such a notion underestimates the influence of the irrational, of animism, magic, and astrology in the life and thought of the seventeenth century, when modern science was in its infancy. And it also distorts the fact that Aristotelian logic and methodology were utilized by the founders of modern science.

We've already begun to suggest the complexity of strands that surrounded Galileo and his contemporaries. Let us now add that, for financial reasons, Galileo had to drop out of the University of Pisa before completing his studies. He continued to study on his own and his work attracted a patron who helped gain him a faculty appointment in mathematics at the University of Pisa in 1589, at the age of 25. He quickly came into conflict with the Aristotelians who ruled the philosophy department there, as they did at most universities. There were several varieties of Aristotelians, distinguished mainly by which commentator on Aristotle they followed (Aquinas, Averroes, or Alexander). In addition, particularly at the Council of Trent, Aristotelian philosophy as utilized by Aquinas was employed as the means of expressing technical definitions and dogmas, thus cloaking that philosophy with the quasi-official mantle of the church. It was, in short, the reigning philosophy and clearly more powerful than the challenge of a junior faculty member in mathematics who did not even have a degree.

Obviously if the Aristotelians were bickering with one another over what Aristotle actually wrote, they had little time for or patience with Galileo's thorny challenges, thus prompting his complaint in 1590: "Few there are who seek to discover whether what Aristotle says is true; it is enough for them that the more texts of Aristotle they have to quote, the more learned they will be thought."[2]

Small wonder that Galileo resigned from Pisa the following year and accepted appointment to the chair of mathematics at the University of Padua, in the Republic of Venice, a post he was to hold for eighteen years. While at Padua, Galileo invented a thermometer, wrote several treatises on mathematics, and became interested in astronomy. Although he wrote Kepler in 1597 that he had discarded the Ptolemaic system years before, recent scholarship has indicated that Galileo's actual acceptance of Copernicanism was more gradual than had previously been thought.[3]

In 1609 Galileo built a telescope that made objects appear nearly one thousand times larger and thirty times closer than when seen with the naked eye. He trained it on the heavens and a year later published his discoveries in a pamphlet entitled *The Starry Messenger*. Its message was a clear challenge both to Ptolemaic astronomy and to some of the cherished tenets of Aristotelian cosmology and physics. He dedicated the work to Cosimo II de Medici, the Grand Duke of Tuscany, who promptly awarded him the chair in mathematics at the University of Pisa. Galileo accepted, but only after his official title was expanded to Ducal Philosopher and Mathematician. No doubt that caused some consternation to his old enemies on the faculty at Pisa.

It is perfectly clear that the initial objections to what Galileo was doing and writing came not from theologians or the Holy Office but from the Aristotelians who clamored to their master's defense. Some of that opposition was comical. Philosopher Lodovico delle Colombe came forward to say that the irregular features Galileo saw on the moon were in fact covered with a smooth, transparent substance, so that the moon was a perfect sphere just as Aristotle had said it was. Others refused to look through the telescope at all, claiming that the mountains were on the lens, not on the moon, and that the quintessence—the perfect matter of the heavens—was safe after all.

But some of the opposition was serious. First, the Copernican system contradicted direct sense experience. Secondly, as Ptolemy had noted, if the earth made a complete turn in twenty-four hours, such tremendous speed would be required that the air, birds, and clouds would all be left behind. In other words, the problem was not simply one of astronomy; a new physics was needed to provide the underpinning for the Copernican system. Thirdly, thanks to a spurious preface by Andreas Osiander, Copernicus was thought to have proposed his system only as a mathematical device for "saving the appearances" in a somewhat simpler way than the Ptolemaic could do. But the strongest argument against the heliocentric system came from Aristotle himself: if the earth moves, stellar displacements or parallaxes would be observable. But none had ever been recorded. That objection was not really answered until 1838 and then only with instruments far more powerful than those possessed by Galileo.

Even with his discovery of the planets of Jupiter, the sunspots, and the phases of Venus, Galileo had no convincing proof *for* the Copernican system. He had some strong challenges to Aristotelian physics and devastating evidence against Ptolemaic astronomy, but all of his discoveries could still be explained within a geostatic universe using the schema of Tycho Brahe, which had the planets revolve around the sun while the sun was revolving around a motionless earth. The Tychonic system, mechanically preposterous as it was, proved to be a heavy feather on Galileo's back.

In 1613 Galileo engaged in an argument with the Jesuit astronomer Christopher Scheiner as to which of them had been first to discover the sunspots. This was probably the first but certainly not the last battle he was to have with a Jesuit. That is of more than minor interest since, as William Wallace has recently detailed, Galileo had derived some early support and many of his methodological principles from Jesuit professors at the Collegio Romano.[4]

But it was philosophy professor Lodovico delle Colombe, not Scheiner, who first used the Bible as a weapon against Galileo. The growing controversy now became a popular subject of discussion. The interest and speculation of experts and amateurs passed from the complex questions of astronomy and physics and came to rest squarely on the scriptural difficulties involved in the new system. People wanted to know how they were to interpret the text of Josh. 10:12-13: "Josue prayed to the Lord, and said in the presence of Israel, 'Stand still, O sun, at Gabaon, O moon, in the valley of Aialon!' And the sun stood still, and the moon stayed, while the nation took vengeance on its foes." Josue would hardly command the sun to stand still if it never moved anyway. Also they wondered how a moving earth and an unmoving sun could be reconciled with the words of the Psalmist, "The Lord is king, in splendor robed; robed is the Lord and girt about with strength; And he has made the world firm, not to be moved" (Ps. 92:1), or with the statement that God "fixed the earth upon its foundation, not to be moved forever" (Ps. 103:5). The Book of Ecclesiastes states that "the sun rises and the sun goes down; then it presses on to the place where it rises" (Eccles. 1:5). Psalm 18 adds its testimony: "He has pitched a tent there for the sun, which comes forth like the groom from his bridal chamber and, like a giant, joyfully runs its course. At one end of the heavens it comes forth, and its course is to the other end" (Ps. 18:6-7). Obviously it was a matter of more than one or two obscure texts. And the context magnified the problem, since scriptural interpretation was the main battlefront between Protestants and Catholics. The Council of Trent had decreed:

> Furthermore, to check unbridled spirits, it (the Holy Council) decrees that no one relying on his own judgment shall, in matters of faith and morals pertaining to the edification of Christian doctrine, distorting the Scriptures in accordance with his own conceptions, presume to interpret them contrary to that sense which holy mother Church, to whom it belongs to judge of their true sense and interpretation, has held and holds, or even contrary to the unanimous teaching of the Fathers, even though such interpretations should never at any time be published.[5]

Galileo's opponents knew what they were doing in forcing a change of venue from physics to theology. Egged on by hearing that a preacher in Florence had given a Sunday sermon condemning the new astronomy and mathematicians in general, Galileo fell into the trap.

We come now to three very crucial documents in the story, each stating a position on biblical hermeneutics vis-à-vis physical science.

The first is by Cardinal Robert Bellarmine, the most powerful theologian in Rome at the time. It is a letter dated April 12, 1615, to Paolo Foscarini, a Carmelite friar who had just published a book attempting to show that the Copernican system is not contrary to Scripture. Bellarmine begins by cautioning Foscarini and Galileo that even if the Copernican system is superior in "saving the appearances," it still should be treated only as a mathematical device and not as something that is real. Secondly, Bellarmine points out that the Council of Trent forbade interpreting Scripture in any way contrary to the agreement of the fathers of the church. And even if the subject matter is not per se a matter of faith or morals, the fact is that all of Scripture is inspired and therefore true, and from that perspective a matter of faith is at stake. Thirdly, he says that if there were a demonstration in favor of the heliocentric system, Scripture would indeed have to be reinterpreted. But "saving the appearances" is not the same as a true demonstration. Short of being forced to change by a real demonstration, the exegesis of the passages in question would not change. In the meantime, the Copernican theory could be treated as a hypothesis, even a superior one. But only proof would necessitate any change in scriptural interpretation.

The second document is by Galileo in the form of a *Letter to the Grand Duchess Christina*, written in 1615.[6] Galileo began by citing Saint Augustine's dictum, "One does not read in the Gospel that the Lord said, 'I will send to you the Holy Spirit who will teach you about the course of the sun and the moon.' For he willed to make them Christians, not mathematicians." Galileo goes on to say that of course the scriptural authors spoke in terms that everyone recognized from common experience. But in physical matters it makes sense to begin not from scriptural texts but from sense experience and necessary demonstrations. So far, so good — in fact, Galileo has written like a better theologian than Bellarmine. But now he falters:

> Yet even in those propositions which are not matters of faith, the authority of Scripture ought to be preferred over that of

all human writings which are supported only by bare assertions or probable arguments and not set forth in a demonstrative way.

He goes on to say:

> From the above words I conceive that I may deduce this doctrine; that in the books of the sages of this world there are contained some physical truths which are soundly demonstrated, and others that are merely stated. As to the former, it is the job of wise theologians to show that they do not contradict the Holy Scriptures. As to the propositions which are stated but not rigorously demonstrated, anything contrary to the Bible involved in them must be held to be undoubtedly false and should be proved so by every possible means.[7]

By granting Scripture strict and exclusive authority over undemonstrated physical arguments to the contrary and by not having demonstrative proof, Galileo loses his own case—but not without an effort to pin down his opponents. He writes:

> Before a physical proposition is condemned it must be shown to be not rigorously demonstrated and this is to be done not by those who hold the proposition to be true, but by those who judge it to be false.[8]

That sounds very much like an attempt to switch the burden of proof. I am of the opinion that Galileo was well aware that he did not have conclusive proof for the Copernican system. But his educated instinct was that someday such proof would be forthcoming. In fact, he had already begun work on his theory of the tides which he believed would soon carry the day. Moreover, he may have felt that asking his opponents to study his evidence closely enough to measure its cogency would bring some of them around to his view.[9] At any rate he would have been better served had he written here what he jotted in the margin of his copy of Bellarmine's *Letter to Foscarini:* "Let those theologians who are not astronomers guard against rendering the Scriptures false by trying to interpret it against propositions which *may* be true and *might* be proven so"[10] (emphasis added).

Galileo did not wait to amass proof; instead he went to Rome to preach Copernicanism in the theologians' front yard. Galileo was justified in believing in mathematical realism and in refusing the "saving the appearances" dodge, but perhaps he should not have forced the issue prematurely. Still there were some important churchmen who were open-minded enough to hear both sides and to seek expert advice. This leads us to the third important document, the *Apologia pro Galileo Mathematico Florentino* by Thomas Campanella, written in 1615 apparently at the request of Cardinal Boniface Gaetani.[11]

Campanella brings several new elements into the story. Although a Dominican, he was an ardent follower of the naturalistic philosophy of Bernardino Telesio. Also, he was at this time serving a prison term in the Fortress of Naples for allegedly plotting the overthrow of the Spanish government there; it appears that all he really did was to use astrology to predict the fall of that government, but in those days that was enough to earn serious reprisals. Thirdly, Campanella was a cheerleader for anything that was anti-Aristotelian and an avowed enemy of anything that could not be "Christianized," a requisite for being included in his utopian City of the Sun. Strangely enough it is this rebel, this undisciplined genius, the author of eighty-eight works—all more than competent but none a classic—who came forth with the solution to the dispute between Bellarmine and Galileo. Had Campanella been listened to, there would have been no Galileo case—at least in the sense that his enemies would not have defeated him using Scripture as their weapon.

The *Apologia* consists of five chapters. In the first chapter, Campanella lists eleven of the arguments used by philosophers and theologians against Galileo. The first two are accusations that Galileo has introduced innovations which contradict Aristotelian philosophy and the unanimous opinion of the fathers of the church. Objections 3–7 are scriptural passages which seem to rule out a heliocentric astronomy. The eighth objection scores as unbelievable Galileo's doctrine that the heavens are corruptible. The next is that he has postulated a plurality of worlds, thereby endangering the dogma of the redemption. Arguments 10–11 *contra* Galileo claim that it is better to renounce novelties than to try to decide questions beyond our capabilities.

In chapter 2, the Dominican records the arguments commonly

cited in support of Galileo. Campanella points out that nearly seventy years had passed since Pope Paul III, to whom Copernicus dedicated his *De revolutionibus orbium caelestium*, approved the work. In those seventy years many great men such as Reinhold, Maestlin, Kepler, Gilbert, and Magini had accepted and advanced the Copernican theory. Thus if it is true that "Galileo has made no additions to the system advanced by Copernicus, and if the *De revolutionibus* does not adversely affect Catholic faith, neither does the work of Galileo" (APG, p. 5).

Another argument for Galileo is that

> because heaven is immobile, Holy Scripture names it the Firmament. The earth therefore must rotate, and the sun stand in the center of the world. As Copernicus and his followers prove and the followers of Ptolemy now admit, this system explains all phenomena and accords with all principles of mathematics. (APG, p. 11)

In this chapter, Campanella is merely reporting the arguments which support the view that the Copernican system should not be prohibited by the church. Campanella was not personally convinced that the new astronomy was the true system of the universe, nor does he try to adduce scientific evidence in its support. His main purpose was to protect Galileo's right to philosophize freely, a cause he espoused because he wanted to see a truly Christian-authored philosophy develop. Why should the works of Copernicus and Galileo, both Catholics, be prohibited in favor of the pagan Aristotle? Campanella notes:

> Because knowledge should be Christian, they lack understanding who forbid and prohibit philosophy among the followers of Christ. They are similar to the Emperor Julian, who outlawed and interdicted all the sciences of the Christians. (APG, p. 25)

Chapter 3 lays down certain indispensable prerequisites for arriving at a solution to the problem. For anyone to be a judge in this matter, he must not only know Holy Scripture and the Fathers, but science as well. Campanella reminds whoever might judge the case that anyone who forbids Christians the study of philosophy and the search for knowledge, likewise forbids them to be Christians. The law of the Christians commends all knowledge to them because they need not fear what is false. (*APG*, p. 25)

He would also have any judge bear in mind that

not all that is false is injurious to Scripture. It must directly or indirectly destroy the true meaning. In addition, if a theologian has advanced doctrines which apparently are equally or more opposed to Holy Scripture than are the theories of Galileo, he is neither condemned nor prohibited from making further inquiry. It is by such inquiry that he determines whether or not the doctrines which he has advanced are sound. He does not thereby impugn faith, but rather, opens truth to the soul. (*APG*, p. 14)

The Dominican friar makes a point of noting that no philosopher or theologian had yet formulated a wholly satisfactory system of the universe, and thus "it is an essential part of the glory of the Christian religion that we permit [Galileo's] method of discovering new knowledge and of correcting the old" (*APG*, p. 26).

He is severely critical of anyone who would make his own unofficial interpretation of Scripture as authoritative as Scripture itself.

I have shown that liberty of thought is more vigorous in Christian countries than it is in other nations. Now if this be true, whoever on his own proscribes limits and laws for human thought and thinks his action is in harmony with the dictates of Holy Scripture, he is not only irrational and dangerous, but irreligious and impious as well. And I say the same of anyone who teaches and accepts no interpretation but his own, and subjects Scripture to his beliefs or to those of some other writer. Such a practice exposes Holy Scripture to the jest of unbelievers and heretics. (*APG*, p. 27)

Using Thomas Aquinas and Augustine as his authorities, he warns against too literal an interpretation of the texts in question.

In the preface to his *Tract against the Errors of the Greeks*, St. Thomas states: "I first assert that many scriptural passages do not pertain to dogmas of faith, but rather to doctrines of philosophy. It does great violence to such passages to affirm or deny them as if they are dogmas." . . . St. Augustine expresses a similar view in the first chapter of his *Commentary on Genesis:* "It is greatly to be guarded against, and is pernicious and shameful for a Christian to speak of physical phenomena as if he were discussing Scripture." . . . It therefore appears to me desirable that we understand that the spheres of philosophy and of our faith do not conflict, and that theories of philosophy are not to be defended as though they were dogmas of faith. (APG, p. 11)

And, Campanella cautions,

If Galileo has demonstrated conclusively the things which he asserts there will ensue among heretics no slight mockery of our Roman theology. This is particularly true since both the heliocentric hypothesis and the telescope have been received with avidity by many men in Germany, France, England, Poland, Denmark, and Sweden. If Galileo's hypothesis is false, it will not disturb theological doctrine, for not all that is untrue is contrary to faith. Indeed if everything false were contrary to faith, our discoveries of the errors made by some Saints when treating of natural philosophy would make them heretics. If Galileo's theory is unsound, it will not endure. I believe therefore that his type of philosophy should not be forbidden. (APG, p. 29)

In chapter 4, Campanella replies to the objections against Galileo which were listed in chapter 1. He points out that many Fathers and Doctors are agreed that sacred Scripture does not supply sufficient evidence on which to construct or prohibit any cosmological system. When an inspired author makes a reference to some physical or astronomical phenomenon, he does not do so to furnish the elements of a scientific theory; he speaks *secundum apparentias*. The message of the Bible is religious, not scientific. Even if the sacred authors had somehow known that the earth moves, prudence would have demanded that they not propound it lest they render their readers incredulous. At any rate, they went by what appeared to their senses. They were in no way making a scientific judgment on the reality of solar motion. It was not their message or their intention to teach astronomy.

No church father, in interpreting these texts, held that the motion of the earth was a matter of faith. As a matter of fact, many Fathers give radically different interpretations to the texts in question. Thus, "neither the Fathers nor the Scholastics definitely concluded that the earth stands still and the heavens are moved" (*APG*, p. 27). What unanimity there is among the Fathers on the motion of the sun comes not from the authority of Scripture or from their desire to consider it as a matter of faith, but is merely the opinion suggested by common sense experience, which has validity so long as science does not bring forth strong arguments to the contrary. Campanella goes on to cite many texts which seem to favor a moving earth. He does this to show the theologians in Rome that the Scripture can be interpreted in support of both sides of the controversy.

In the fifth and final chapter, Campanella examines the arguments presented in favor of Galileo in chapter 2. Campanella admits that in some of his writings he had tried to refute the arguments of Pythagoras and Copernicus. And he confesses that since Galileo's discoveries he has had to change a number of his opinions. But he still has his reservations with regard to the new astronomy. "The hypothesis of Copernicus and Galileo is probable, not true (i.e., not demonstrated)" (*APG*, p. 54). In his *Metaphysics*, composed almost entirely during his imprisonment, the Dominican friar held for a geocentric system. In an appendix to this work, he added in 1626 an account of Galileo's discoveries and said that he did this so that if Galileo's doctrines were true, the Catholic faith would not be mocked as not even knowing them. Also, Campanella had written to Galileo in 1610 to tell him that he was thrilled by the Florentine scientist's great discoveries. But he advised Galileo that, in his opinion, "many Copernican doctrines will have to be changed by you." Campanella very probably considered the Copernican system to be a solid theory backed by empirical evidence. But he did not come out in unqualified support of it. This was not because he feared the church, but because he was not completely convinced it was true. He concluded the *Apologia* by saying: "It is unnecessary that the investigations of Galileo be suppressed, a misfortune which is about to occur. Our enemies will seize eagerly on this action and proclaim it abroad" (*APG*, p. 57).

CONCLUSION

The *Apologia* has its logical flaws, a subjective prejudice against everything Aristotelian, and several theological wanderings. But on the whole, it is an amazing document. It contains a workable solution for all apparent discrepancies between Scripture and science. Campanella holds that any scientific theory which directly or indirectly is opposed to a doctrine of faith must be condemned. For example, a mechanistic conception of human beings which excludes an immortal soul could be condemned on the authority of Scripture. But any passage of Scripture whose meaning has not been infallibly defined by the church or unanimously interpreted by the Fathers as a matter of faith is open to more than one possible interpretation. Now it is true that a tradition of accepted exegesis and the common agreement of theologians can give a probable meaning to a text. But unless this interpretation is defined by the church or is the unanimous exegesis of the Fathers who explicitly declare it to be a matter of faith, it remains a fallible, however probable, interpretation.

Applying this to the case at hand, we can see how the theologians could and should have reconciled the new astronomy with the sacred Scriptures. Since Scripture does not intend to teach science, it is not to be appealed to as establishing one astronomical system or forbidding another. Not one father of the church thought that the geocentric system was a matter of faith. That every word of the Scriptures is true is a matter of faith. But the Galileo issue was not a question of the truth of Scripture. The issue was, What does Scripture mean in the passages where it seems to affirm that the sun moves and the earth stands still? A tradition of geocentric interpretation of the texts demanded respect, but not the adherence of faith. It should have been considered as the more probable exegesis. The opposing interpretation would then have been possible but less probable. In any case no one should risk censure for offering alternative interpretations of the texts in question. As proof for the Copernican hypothesis developed, the new interpretation, namely that Scripture was not affirming a geocentric system, would have grown in probability until it eventually became the more probable interpretation. In this way Scripture would not have to be reinterpreted to meet every new hypothesis, nor would science be forced to bow before an unjustified commitment of theologians to a text which was not meant to teach science.

The influence in Rome of Campanella's *Apologia* was negligible. Time was too short and Campanella himself too suspect to command the respect of a board bent on orthodoxy. An unfortunate decree was issued by the Congregation of the Index on March 5, 1616, characterizing the Copernican view as false and contrary to holy Scripture and prohibiting Copernicus' *De revolutionibus orbium caelestium* "until corrected." Galileo was given a private admonition from the Holy Office not to defend or teach his position. As long as the decree of 1616 stayed on the books, Galileo had to do his science while walking a theological tightrope. Finesse was never his forte. In 1633, Galileo was condemned vehemently, suspected of heresy for attempting to prove, in his *Dialogue on the Two Great Systems of the World*, that the earth moves. Many factors were involved, of course, but these unjust decisions of 1616 and 1633 could have been avoided if the theologians in Rome had listened to Campanella.

With the discovery of more scientific evidence in favor of a heliocentric universe, the prohibitions against Copernican writings were eventually revoked. But the damage had already been done. For more than three hundred years, polemics have been written, as Campanella predicted they would be, denouncing the church as the sworn enemy of science and progress.

Moreover, in another fascinating and unfortunate reversal of roles, by the end of the seventeenth century science had become the new orthodoxy and the metaphysicians and theologians were allowed only to fill in the gaps. Where formerly Galileo's opponents had dismissed his arguments on faulty, a priori grounds, now the mechanists picked up the univocal wand and waved teleology, theology, and even chance out of the universe.

We seem, in our time, to have come a long way from all of these brands of dogmatism. By now we know, of course, that science, though a powerful source of knowledge and understanding, is only one of many ways of coming to know and respond to reality.

By now we know how complex all of history really is. One could spend a lifetime tracing just the obvious influences at work in the Galileo case. Imagine if we add the personal jealousies and animosities or look at the case that Redondi has built that the condemnation had nothing to do with astronomy and Scripture—that it was an attempt by the Jesuits to protect the hylomorphic explanation of the Eucharist from Galileo's atomism. On the other hand, one could also build a fairly convincing case that Pope Urban VIII turned against Galileo in 1633 because he believed that Galileo was a friend of a well-known astrologer who was publicly predicting Urban's death.[12] Clearly, the facts lend themselves to widely different interpretations, showing that historical interpretation too must often rest on one or another degree of probability.

By now we understand the need for orthodoxy in the creedal profession of faith. But there are still disputes about what is properly an object of faith and what is not. Contemporary attempts to denounce the theory of evolution on religious grounds are a reminder that the demand for absolutes ignores at its own peril the vast and valid range of probability that frames most of our knowledge and even some of our belief.

Finally, it is sad to see a resurgence of the inquisitorial mentality in Rome. The condemnation and silencing of liberation theologians in Latin America and the removal of Hans Küng and Charles Curran from Catholic faculties of theology clearly indicate that Rome is still unwilling to respond to doctrinal differences by careful and measured argumentation rather than authoritative confrontation.

History is ignored at one's own peril. Perhaps we have not come as far as we think we have. It is obvious that the Galileo case has much to teach us about freedom. It is obvious as well that we still have much to learn.

NOTES

1. Pietro Redondi, *Galileo: Heretic* (Princeton, N.J.: Princeton University Press, 1987).

2. Galileo, *De motu*, cited by F. S. Taylor, *Galileo and the Freedom of Thought* (London: Watts, 1938), p. 39.

3. See Robert S. Westman, "The Copernicans and the Churches," in *God and Nature*, ed. David C. Lindberg and Ronald L. Numbers (Berkeley: University of California Press, 1986), pp. 76–113.

4. William A. Wallace, *Galileo and His Sources* (Princeton, N.J.: Princeton University Press, 1984).

5. H. J. Schroeder, ed., *Canons and Decrees of the Council of Trent* (St. Louis: Herder, 1941), p. 18.

6. For a thorough analysis see Jean Dietz Moss, "Galileo's Letter to Christina," *Renaissance Quarterly* 36, no. 4 (Winter 1983): 547–76. Another view is that of Maurice Finocchiaro, "The Methodological Background to Galileo's Trial," in *Reinterpreting Galileo*, ed. William A. Wallace (Washington: Catholic University Press, 1986), pp. 241ff.

7. "Letter to the Grand Duchess Christina," *Le Opere di Galileo Galilei*, ed. A. Favaro (Florence: Barbera, 1890–1909), vol. 5, pp. 309ff. Translated in Stillman Drake, *Discoveries and Opinions of Galileo* (New York: Doubleday, 1957), pp. 175ff.

8. Cited in Drake, *Discoveries and Opinions of Galileo*, p. 194.

9. In support of this interpretation see William R. Shea, "Galileo and the Church," in *God and Nature*, ed. Lindberg and Numbers, p. 127.

10. Cited in Drake, *Discoveries and Opinions of Galileo*, p. 168.

11. Thomas Campanella, *Apologia pro Galileo* (Frankfurt, 1622), trans. Grant McColley, *Smith College Studies in History*, vol. 22, nn. 3–4 (1937). I have modified this translation where necessary. Hereafter referred to as *APG*.

12. See L. S. Lerner and E. A. Gosselin, "Galileo and the Specter of Bruno," *Scientific American*, November, 1986, pp. 126–33. This article attempts to show that Galileo was tried partly because his arms were mistakenly identified with those of Giordano Bruno. They fail to prove their case, but their effort is one more proof that the facts can be assembled in support of novel and competing theses.

8
Freedom as Action in Indian Philosophy
J. N. MOHANTY

A THEORY OF ACTION FORMS the cornerstone for practical philosophy, and this is true of Indian thought as well. Legal thought and ritualistic speculations, ethical and spiritual philosophies — all center around a theory of action. Even those spiritual philosophies which recommend inaction or transcendence of action in any of a whole variety of senses make use, in doing so, of certain widely held ideas of what action is all about. Some clarification about the concept of action is fundamental to understanding Indian thought, and yet it is still one of the neglected topics in modern writings in this field. With this general introduction we may now turn to our topic.

I

A theory of action would inevitably cut across psychology, semantics, and ontology before it takes us into practical philosophy. A rather preliminary schematic analysis of an action yields the following factors: agent (*karta*); knowledge; desire to act (*cikirsa* or *icchā*); and effort (*pravṛtti*). We can begin by looking at each of these.

1. Agent or *karta:* Panini defines the (grammatical) agent or *karta* by the idea of independence. One is independent who is *kriyanukulakrtiman*, that is, possesses *krti*, or will, which is conducive to the action. That person is the locus of the will to act

(*vyapara*) which is the meaning of the verbal root. In the sentences "The jar arises," "The jar will be destroyed," the jar is not the primary (*mukhya*) agent even if it is the grammatical subject, for it does not possess independence in the sense defined.

2. Knowledge: The knowledge that is relevant in the context of action theory consists of (a) the cognition that something is to be done (*karyatajnana*); (b) the cognition that it can be done (*krtisadhyatajnana*); and (c) the cognition that some good will come out of doing it (*istasadhanatajnana*). The cognition is not simple cognition of a fact but rather of an act — not as given but as something to be done.

There is an important difference with regard to (c): the Nyāya school emphasizes it while the Prabhakara Mīmāṁsākas want to do away with it. The difference is really due to their different views about whether a sense of duty is to be motivated by a desire for some good consequence or not. On the Nyāya analysis, I do what I do because I recognize that I can do it and that it is the only means to attaining some good. On the Mīmāṁsā analysis, I do what is enjoined in the moral code (of the Scriptures) when I represent the enjoined action as a qualification of myself (that is, I represent myself as doing it) and I recognize that the said actions are to be done by me. On the Nyāya view, nothing is striven after, desired, save in relation to the agent, and this self-relation is a consciousness of good. On the Mīmāṁsā view, self-reference is not necessarily a consciousness of good. We have a sort of distinction between consequentialism and deontologism in moral theory, or rather in action theory in general.

3. Desire to act or *icchā*: One definition of desire (*icchā*) is that it is what is directly conducive to volition (*pravrtteh saksadanukulatvam*). As a rather well-known verse runs, "Desire is due to the self (*atmajanya bhavediccha*) while volition is due to desire (*icchājanya bhaverkrtih*)." The desire to do leads to

4. Volition or *krti*. This desire moves the will to put forth actual effort unless there is a powerful counteracting aversion (*dveṣa*). This leads to *yatna* or motor effort, whose general meaning is "cessation of passivity" (*udasinatva-viccheda*). The result of this motor effort is the action itself or *karya*. The verse quoted earlier ends like this: "Effort is due to volition (*krtijanya bhavechesta*); the action is due to effort (*cestajanya bhavet kriya*)."

To complete this brief sketch, let us recall that the Bhatta Mīmāmsākas distinguished between two kinds of volition (or *pravrtti*): those that are spontaneous or self-caused (*svarasiki*) and those that are imposed (*prairaniki*). The self-caused ones are the ones that are caused by the cognition of what is to be done as conducive to good; the imposed ones are: in ordinary contexts (*loke*) commands of secular authorities such as the monarch, and in religious contexts (*vede*) the imperative sentences of the Scriptures. It is only the last which are strictly ethical. Those that are caused by the knowledge of conduciveness to a good are hypothetical imperatives, rules of prudence. Those that are "imposed" by commands of secular authorities (such as the sovereign) are in accordance with law; only those that are imposed by the imperatives of the Scriptures are, strictly speaking, ethical.

In the latter two cases, what prompts a person to act is the simple imperative form of the sentence. The imperative sentence, or *vidhi*, is often defined as the sentence which brings about volition. There is ample discussion in the Mīmāmsā literature as to how the grammatical form of an imperative is conducive to volition — into the details of which I need not enter for my present purpose.

In the light of the foregoing, I may say — following Vacaspati — that agency or *kartrtva* is the coinherence of cognition, desire, volition, and effort. One who desires and even wills without knowledge of the means adopted and its operations should not be called an agent; nor should one be so called if she or he desires but, owing to laziness, makes no effort.

Does this above analysis of action — agreed upon in its general outline by the various schools of Indian philosophy — entail "freedom of the will"? The cognition "I can do," which is a cause of the appropriate desire, may be regarded as a psychological evidence for freedom. But at the same time, the desire and the volition are also caused by the cognition of the proposed action's conduciveness to good, or simply by the force of the imperative command of the sovereign or of the Scriptures. It is indeed difficult to ascertain whether the Hindu philosophers subscribed to freedom of the will or not. In order to be able to decide this issue, we must first ascertain whether the Hindu philosophers had the Western concept of will or not. One cannot just assume that this latter concept was available, that it is a purely phenomenological-descriptive concept without theological-metaphysical and historicocultural determinations. One thing appears undeniable: the Hindu and the Buddhist philosophers did not have the tripartite faculty psychology so familiar in classical Western thought. Volition was often a function of *buddhi*, often of *Manas* or *antahkarana* (the inner sense). If the same concept of will was not available, the problem of freedom could not have been the same — also because the problem of freedom arose in Western thinking in the context of the theological idea of divine omnipotence and foreknowledge.

II

A philosophy of action may take various forms. Besides the psychological analysis which the just-recalled Hindu theory embodies, philosophy of action may be either phenomenological or metaphysical. I will briefly sketch two examples, one of each, and then proceed to reflect on the Hindu thinking on action using them as foils.

For a quasi-phenomenological account, let me turn to Hannah Arendt's book *The Human Condition*. Arendt's theory is of what she calls action as distinguished from labor and work. While labor is "prescribed by the biological process of the living organism" and work produces an "artificial" world of things, different from all natural surroundings, action in Arendt's sense goes on among people.[1] Labor assures maintenance of life; work produces human artifacts (tools, works of art); only action makes politics and history possible.

Action presupposes a community and is not done in isolation. It also requires speech. Without speech, action cannot reveal its doer, and an action without its doer is meaningless, while an art work remains what it is whether or not we know the artist's name. To act, further, is to take an initiative, to begin (*archein*), to set something in motion. Each action makes a new beginning. For Arendt, this corresponds to the fact of birth. It starts a new process "which eventually emerges as the unique life story of the newcomer."[2] Although each action aims at a purpose, the "existing web of . . . innumerable, conflicting wills and intentions"[3] makes it unlikely that it ever achieves its purpose. The "stories" that it does produce, however, go beyond the intention of the actor. As a consequence, the eventual outcome of one's actions is never the agent her- or himself. It is as though "an invisible hand behind the scene" determines the outcome, so that humankind often seems to be a plaything of a god, as Arendt notes, quoting Plato.[4] The doer is also a sufferer. In view of the endless consequences beyond human foresight, the old virtue of moderation makes sense. One truly understands an action only at the end, when, as Arendt puts it, all participants are dead. To put it another way, human essence comes into being only with death — not for the agent but for those who will tell his or her story.

Arendt's account emphasizes the intersubjectivity of action as well as the intention and will of the agent. At the same time, it reminds us of the unforeseeable causal chain that an act releases, of the tragedy of being responsible for consequences one did not anticipate, and of the hope that with death one's life story will be complete and thereby one's essential being "constituted" for the first time.

Contrast this with Hegel's remarks on action in the Jena *Phenomenology*. Again, Hegel is speaking of action in the sense of ethical action. Ethical consciousness, as self-consciousness, is the pure and simple directedness toward the essential principle of ethical life. It is consciousness of doing one's duty. It knows what it has to do. However, without its knowing, this self-certainty of ethical consciousness is destroyed by (1) the conflict between human and divine law, and (2) the conflict between knowledge and ignorance. In Hegel's terminology, human law is the explicit law of the society. The divine law is the hidden law of the family. The case of Antigone typifies the conflict between the two. On the other hand, the case of Oedipus shows how, in Hegel's words, "a hidden power shunning the light of day waylays the ethical self-consciousness, a power which bursts forth only after the deed is done and seizes the doer in the act."[5] Thus, in every deed a conscious certainty of one's intentions, principles, and goals is bound up with what is alien and external. But this external reality is also due to the deed itself. Hence "the act is itself this diremption . . . establishing over against this an alien external reality. That such a reality exists is due to the deed itself, and is the outcome of it."[6]

Destiny in the *Phenomenology*, according to Hyppolite, manifests the interior self exteriorly.

III

In the light of these philosophies, we may turn to the Hindu idea of *karma*. It is well known that the idea of *karma*, with its associated ideas of rebirth and *mokṣa* as deliverance from rebirth, constitutes one of the most distinctive features of Hindu religious and philosophical thinking. What I am here trying to do is to understand some fragments of this deep conceptual structure, and to interpret its bearing on such familiar concepts as freedom.

We have followed both Arendt and Hegel, taking us beyond the limits of the phenomenological consciousness of the agent as the actor. Strictly phenomenologically, an action has for its agent what Schutz called "subjective meaning." The agent knows what she is doing, what her intention and intended consequences are. He may even have the consciousness of having chosen to do what he does. However, this phenomenological consciousness, though valid within limits—for example, within the "reduced" domain of how the action is presented to the agent in consciousness and with the real existential constraints bracketed out—soon comes to grief. Not only does the most rational of agents fail to anticipate —and even retrospectively to rationally reconstruct—all the consequences of her action, but, as Arendt insists, the story cannot be complete before she is dead. As both Arendt and Hegel realized, the agent's own actions may turn back upon him as an alien power, as destiny in Arendt's case, owing to the complicated web of other people's wills and intentions, and in Hegel's case owing to the so-called divine law and the laws of unconscious human nature of which the actor is unaware. The point, however, is that the chain of consequences of one's actions recede linearly into the remote horizon, never to be recovered by the agent in her own lifetime, but also vertically into dimensions from where they can surface, looking like alien powers.

The Hindus, as also the Buddhists, realized this more clearly than any others. They also realized this situation in its extreme logical consequence and sought to understand and bear with it in all its fearful and awesome possibilities. We have, however, gone beyond phenomenology into metaphysics.

How does this metaphysics of action and that phenomenology tie together? The connections are not difficult to see. If all action is caused by desire, as our preliminary analysis pointed out, and if all desire to act is caused by the belief that it will bring about a satisfying state (*iṣṭasadhanata*), the only consequences that the Hindu thinkers admitted into their theory were states in which desires are either fulfilled or frustrated. All other consequences are reduced to these, not denied. Actions bring about either *sukha* or *duhkha*. The chain of consequences that recede beyond the reaches of phenomenological inspection are such states. But such states cannot float in the air; they need a habitat that is capable of conscious experience and one which is, in some sense, identical with the agent.

While such is the connecting link, the conceptual ties are not all that tight. There are indeed loose ends. For example, why assume that all consequences, even those that follow the death of the agent, are of the nature of *sukha* and *duhkha* without covertly presupposing that an identical self survives as the habitat of such experiences? But nowhere in the transition from a phenomenology to a metaphysics are the conceptual links that tight. One expects rational intelligibility, but not rational acceptance. The *karma* theory is a metaphysical theory *par excellence*, based upon a phenomenology of action, not following from it deductively. As a metaphysical theory, it is capable of neither empirical confirmation nor empirical disconfirmation. Its appraisal has to be practical. How does the belief transform one's overall view of life? What meaning does it impart to one's vocations, decisions, and choices, to one's rights and obligations and aspirations, to one's relations to others and to the world at large? These are issues into which I cannot enter, but before returning to the allied concepts of *dharma* and *mokṣa*, let me take this opportunity to warn against certain hasty and easily available misjudgments.

IV

One such widely held view is that the Hindu theory in some way involves "eternal recurrence," and so, by implication, a conception of cyclic time. Paul Tillich even argued that with eternal recurrence there would be no *mokṣa*, for the state of *karma* would have to recur, so that all one's efforts at *mokṣa* would be in vain. It would be another story to show how and why certain doctrines in the Hindu philosophies — and even more so, certain themes in the *purāṇas* — got misinterpreted into the so-called cyclic view of time and then contrasted with the Judeo-Christian linear view of it. That the Hindu view of time was not cyclic has been well documented.

Another such view, understandable in its origin and less wide of the mark, is that the theory of *karma* involves determinism. If one's actions in the past lives determine one's situation in this, then it may seem as though one is not free to change one's situation; one is already predetermined to be what one is. This, however, is only seemingly so. In truth, what determines one's situation is one's own past actions, and likewise what gives shape to one's future is one's present choices. These latter, however — and this is the truth about the charge of determinism — are not totally free choices as though they are made by a transcendental ego. At any time, my situation, determined by my past choices, has already been carved out, and the present choices are from within this determinate horizon. If I can never be totally free, neither am I totally determined. My life is an interplay of determination and freedom.

Even as I say this, I must add several remarks so that we do not jump to hasty conclusions. In the first place, the standard Western deterministic theories have in view such objective impersonal and collective determinants as physical and cultural environments, historical and economic conditions, bodily processes, etc. It is only the psychoanalytic determinism which has some inkling of the way one's own past but infantile experiences, operating within one's own psyche, may give shape to one's present mental life; but most philosophers who have thought about it in the context of the problems of freedom and responsibility have satisfied themselves that this sort of determination is compatible with freedom, moral responsibility, and legal culpability. Karmic determinism is along this line, but radicalizes it still further and should be much less repugnant to the idea of freedom and responsibility.

There is one point, however, with respect to which comparison of karmic with psychoanalytic determinism is misleading. The point of the comparison was that both are internal determinisms. In both cases, it is my past experiences and their traces within my psyche which determine my present. However, while this is clearly true of psychoanalytic determinism, it is not that clearly true of karmic determinism. For one thing, in the case of karmic determination there is a systematic ambiguity in the applications of the words *I* and *my* across different lives. *I* applies to each member of the series of lives in a unique sense, and there appears none who calls them all "mine." If I am J. N. M., and the past life which was "mine" be A. N. B., I cannot now say that A. N. B. was "I" in the same sense in which J. N. M. is so; I cannot say A. N. B. was "my" past life in the same sense in which the infancy of J. N. M. was my infancy. It is only if some one could remember all those past lives as having been one's own that one could have a sense of *I* and *mine* which is different from the way we use those indexicals on sundry, mundane occasions. If that is so, then even if "my" past life determines my present, that determination is ambiguous, as between a purely external determination and a purely intrapsychic determination.

The nature of this determination, the causation involved, is also different from naturalistic causation on the one hand and intentional causation on the other. The Indian theoreticians had to take recourse to the idea of supersensible "traces" (*saṁskāras*) to make sense of translife causality. What is important, then, is to keep in mind that this could not be causal explanation in the sense of a covering law. Nor could it have been arrived at by an inductive generalization, for ordinary experience could not provide data regarding the causation involved. My purpose is not to make the situation, along with its mystery, any more intelligible than it is. I wish to say only how it is *not* to be understood. There is no karmic science; there is a karmic metaphysical point of view. And this point of view, unless misconstrued as a scientific or pseudoscientific determinism, is compatible with the introspective sense, "I could have done otherwise."

V

It is often said that Hindu ethics knows only of duties, but not of rights. If this is a limitation, it characterizes much ethical thinking in the West as well, notably the Kantian. You cannot remedy it simply by saying that once you have duties, you can derive rights from them — for example, if it is one's duty to respect life, a living being must have a right to life — because this deduction does not always work. It is the duty of a *kṣatriya*, for example, to defend a righteous cause. From this duty no right accrues to any one. Even where it does work, consciousness of duty need not entail consciousness of right. Rights such as are embodied in the American constitution are products of modern consciousness.

The Hindu thinkers of antiquity assigned duties to ethics and rights to law. The word *dharma* includes both. *Dharma-śāstra* includes both ethics and law. The latter is often demarcated as *vyavhara*, but that is applied specifically in the context of court action. I will first say a word about Hindu law before moving along to *dharma* in the strict sense and finally to *mokṣa*.

Law: One exemplary misinterpretation of oriental thought was Hegel's view that, in the Orient, only one is free — that is, the despot. Professor Tambiah of Harvard has gone into interesting details about the source of Hegel's information. To see how mistaken Hegel was, note that the best authorities on ancient Hindu law held that the monarch was not the source of the law. Rather, the judicial authority of the monarch was based not on the fiction of monarchical divinity but on positive law and the sovereign's role as military chief. The Austinian conception of positive law as command of the sovereign was never recognized. Every law, as Sengupta argued, was *dharma* and had its alleged justification in the supposedly eternal principles, as well as in right conduct according to current conceptions of right. The monarch was supposed to be the guardian of law, rather than the source of it. The sources of law are said to be the Scriptures, tradition, good custom, and *atma-tusti* (inner contentment or approval of conscience). As Lingat notes, there is no reference in any of the commentaries and digests to the laws or ordinances passed by any historical monarch. The sovereign cannot interfere either with *dharma* or with custom (*ācāra*). The monarch can, according to *Narada* 18.9, reform unreasonable laws and, according to *Katyayana* 42, abolish customs repugnant to reason. However, *Brh* 2.28 wants the monarch not to touch custom.

In saying that in legal theory the sovereign had no power

over law, I do not imply that powerful, despotic monarchs did not surpass their authority. What I wish to emphasize is that the one alone was not free. If the concrete medium of freedom was law, as Hegel himself held to be the case, the Hindu society had a good measure of that objective freedom.

Property is an example of philosophical concern with legal right. The Hindu legal philosophers wrote extensively on this concept. The classic work is the logician Raghunātha Siromani's *Svatvavicara*.[7] A familiar definition of property argues that *svatva*, or being one's own property, equals *yathesta-viniyoga-yogyatva*, that is, the capacity for using the thing at one's own pleasure. However, since law did not permit any and every use, others amended the definition to understand property as a thing that is morally and legally fit to be used at pleasure. Going through a series of such definitions, Raghunātha settles upon a subjective one: it is an impression produced in the mind by the cognition "This is mine." There were obvious problems, for property rights may belong to infants and lunatics, which required rejecting a purely subjective concept in favor of an objective, relational definition. In any event, I trust that this brief sketch will suffice to displace many a persistent misunderstanding.

VI

Now we come to the theory of *dharma*. I will not enter into the issues arising out of the familiar multiple meanings of the word *dharma* and will not speculate on the relations between these meanings. Suffice it to say that the word has three principal uses: (1) the essence of a thing ("the *dharma* of a fire is to burn"); (2) the harmonious order of the cosmos; and (3) injunctions and prohibitions as stated in the Scriptures and law books. The Hindu mind obviously saw a relation between these three senses. At the same time, it is easy to be tempted by a rather simplified picture of that relationship.

For my purpose it is the third meaning which is relevant. Even in this meaning, *dharma* includes a great variety of rules and codes: legal, religious, ritualistic, and ethical. Is it proper, and if so in what sense, to characterize *dharma* as ethical code?

Various definitions of *dharma* are presented in the classical philosophical and *Dharma*-literature:

1. Jaimini's *Mīmāṁsāsutra: dharma* is of the nature of an injunction (*codanalaksanortho*)
2. Kanada's *Vaisesikasutra: dharma* is that from which prosperity and the highest good come about (*yato'bhyudayanihsreyasasiddhih*)
3. The Veda: *dharma* is the goal to be attained (*apadevi*)

Thus, according to the Hindu tradition, *dharma* in the strict sense, excluding the law codes and rules of polity, is expressed by injunctive sentences of the Vedas. The later *dharma-śāstras* clarify, expound, and explain them. These injunctions embody rules that are of various sorts. They may be obligatory or occasional. They may pertain to one's *varna* (caste) or to one as a member of a family (*kula*), or they may be for all humans (*sadharana*). Many of them pertain to a person's role and status in society, but this is not true of all of them. The so-called *sadharana* or common *dharmas* are not so. What is common to them all is that they are all expressed in imperatives.

Are they ethical rules? Was there a Hindu ethics? If we leave out legal, political, and economic rules and focus on the core of traditional Hindu moral codes, do we have there what should be called an ethics?

Two considerations weigh against an affirmative answer. In the first place, many of the rules have the form of hypothetical imperatives. Only the so-called *sadharana dharmas* are not formulated in hypothetical form. Secondly, what we have is a seemingly motley crowd of codes. No attempt is made to unify them in a system or deduce them from a principle.

The core codes, if hypothetical in form, are correlated to consequences which are transworldly. The philosophers who thought about these injunctions came up with two alternative answers as to whether they are to be construed consequentialistically or deontically. Badari and, following him, Krishna in the *Gita*, gave deontic interpretations. The injunctions are to be followed as duties; the consequences stated are not intended to be motivating factors. Jaimini gave a consequentialist reading: "If you desire such and such consequences, then. . . ." Thus, while a very important strand in Hindu thinking is Kantian, the mere presence of consequentialism should not be construed as ruling out the idea of a Hindu ethics, for the idea of ethics does not analytically imply Kantian deontic theory.

Secondly, an important feature of Hindu thinking on *dharma* is that the injunctions embodying *dharma* were never theologically grounded. The *dharma*-imperatives are not commands of God or gods; nor are they commands of political sovereigns. They are autonomous in the sense that they have their source in verbal instructions, not in any premise about facts. The *ought* is kept independent of *is*. This is the basis of the oft-advanced claim that the *dharmas* are grounded in *śabda-pramāṇa*, the claim that the only source of our cognition of moral rules is the language of imperative sentences.

Third, not all moral theories are monistic, unifying rules into a system, or deducing them from a principle. It is only in modern times that this mode of thinking came to prevail. The virtue ethics of antiquity was pluralistic.

Fourth, I want to distinguish, following Hegel once again, between *Sittlichkeit* and *Moralität* and to maintain that, in Hegel's sense, Hindu ethics concerned *Sittlichkeit*. It was not *Moralität* in the modern, Kantian sense. Read Hegel's account of the Greek ethical world where everyone knew for certain what she or he had to do. The laws are familiar and recognized by everyone in a natural ethical community. The Hindu *Sittlichkeit*, as expressed in the Scriptures, was meant to be such.

However, as Hegel pointed out, so also here, this seamless unity of *Sittlichkeit* is soon broken asunder by internal conflicts—not only between *dharma* and the idea of spiritual freedom (*mokṣa*), but between different domains of *dharma*, as the *Gita* illustrates: between *varṇasrama dharma* and *kuladharma*. In Hegel's thinking, it was also the conflict between the social ethos and the laws of family that broke the unity of the Greek ethical world.

VII

The ideal of *mokṣa* transcends the claims of *dharma*. The conflict between the two pervades the history of Hindu thought as much as attempts to resolve the conflict. *Mokṣa* is construed differently in different systems of Hindu thought, but no matter what concept of it one takes into account, the conflict and the tension remain. One may want to resolve the conflict in any of the following ways:

1. Make *mokṣa* itself into a *dharma*, and give it a higher rank in comparison with other *dharmas*.
2. Make *dharma*, or a life in accordance with *dharmas*, a means to and preparation for, even if not the immediate antecedent of, attainment of *mokṣa*.
3. Take away the claim of *dharma* to be absolute. *Mokṣa* transcends the realm of *dharma*, of moral good and evil. There is a radical cleavage separating the two discourses.

Orthodoxy chose either or both of (1) and (2). It argued that *dharma* as embodied in the words of the Scriptures had absolute validity even for the person who attained *mokṣa*. Without it, there is no *mokṣa*. Śaṁkara gave good arguments why *mokṣa* is not *dharma*. It is not an action whose performance could be enjoined. It is rather a state of being, consequent upon knowing the truth. The philosophical issue turns on whether knowledge can be the subject matter for an imperative ("You ought to know").

Liberalism rejected (1) and (2) and opted for (3). Morals are relative and changeable. You need some *dharma* or other for social cohesion. But there is no absolutely valid set of *dharmas*. The *varṇasrama dharma* or *Sittlichkeit* based on *varṇa* has played out its role and needs to be replaced by another. There is no direct transition from *dharma* to *mokṣa* but rather a Kierkegaardian leap.

Orthodoxy, however, did perceive a truth. You do not want a person who has achieved *mokṣa* to be an unrighteous person. You would reasonably expect his or her actions to be in conformity with some reasonable ethical system more internally coherent than that in common use.

What then is the point of saying that the person who has achieved *mokṣa* is beyond the distinction between good and evil? Krishna says this in the *Gita*. To say that such a person can do anything whatsoever—such as a heinous crime—with impunity or rather with spiritual splendor is counterintuitive. One expects such a person to be righteous in an important sense. He or she may not be in conformity with the caste-*dharma*, or family-*dharma*, but such a one will continue to abide by the universal *dharma* of truth, nonviolence, and doing good to others. Why is one *beyond* good and evil? Would the Kantian distinction between good will and holy will help us? The ordinary person follows *dharmas* because the Scriptures command them. The liberated person follows only that *dharma* which is consistent with self-knowledge and practices it with inner spontaneity—not as following rules.

NOTES

1. Hannah Arendt, *The Human Condition* (Chicago: University of Chicago Press, 1958), p. 98.
2. Ibid., p. 184.
3. Ibid.
4. Ibid., p. 185.
5. Hegel *Jena Phenomenology* 490.
6. Hegel *Jena Phenomenology* 488.
7. An English exposition of this work is to be found in J. Duncan Derrett, *Essays in Classical and Modern Hindu Law* (Leiden: E. J. Brill, 1976), pp. 333–57.

PART III

Freedom in Society

9
Social Structures and Structural Ethics
LOUIS DUPRÉ

I. THE SOCIAL CHARACTER OF PREMODERN ETHICS

VALÉRY'S FAMOUS REMARK THAT a poem is never finished, but merely abandoned, pertains no less to the history of ideas. The issues which perplex philosophers are seldom definitively resolved. Such seems the fate of the classical ethical ideal of the common good, whose eclipse heralded the rise of the new, contractual school of natural law in the seventeenth and eighteenth centuries. Of the great ethical insights of the Aristotelian, Stoic, and Scholastic traditions in which the virtuous life presumed the "bonum commune," there would remain only "flawed words and stubborn sounds."[1]

The new national states developed independently of the kind of ethical speculation that had guided political thinkers in the past. With the waning of the classical conception of ethics, morality was reduced to the private sphere and the reign of *Realpolitik* began. It is the lasting merit of Machiavelli to have articulated clearly the new state of mind. Admonishing the prince to be "a great feigner and dissembler," Machiavelli is less a moral apostate than a prescient observer of the limits of morality in shaping the modern state, where "men are so simple and so ready to obey present necessities, that one who deceives will always find those who allow themselves to be deceived."[2] In the rare and heady air of a world despoiled of limits, everything was permissible.

The infamy of the prophet of *verità effettuale* in politics is exceeded only by the emulation of that prophet. For "Machiavelli," writes Croce, "discovered the necessity and the autonomy of politics, politics which is beyond moral good and evil, which has its own laws against which it is futile to rebel."[3] Yet if Machiavelli's splendid amorality is a form of cynicism, heeding his critique is the beginning of ethical wisdom. Indeed, the dissolution of the classical motifs of the *jus naturale* owes its origins less to Machiavelli than to late Scholastic nominalism, which envisioned the will of the commander, divine or human, rather than the intrinsic rationality of the rule as the formal element of law. Of this patrimony, *The Prince* is the denouement, occasioned by the dismal political situation of Machiavelli's Florence.

Centuries of political pragmatism have not dimmed the relevance of the question posed by Machiavelli — the question, in Thomas Nagel's words, of "the nature of the discontinuity between individual morality and public morality";[4] or, in those of Stuart Hampshire, of the relation "between political violence and political deceit on the one side and, on the other, the minimal acceptable moral standards which define human decency."[5] Philosophers like Nagel and Hampshire have seriously begun to reconsider social ethics on a basis differing from medieval natural law, to be sure, yet differing even more from presently reigning theories which confine morality to the private domain. My reflections should be read in light of these attempts.

While for Aristotle virtuous activity is an end in itself, *praxis* rather than *poiēsis*, for modern moralists as diverse as R. M. Hare and John Rawls morality is itself a "poetic" construction. Moral theory is generated as prudentially self-interested choice and subject to formally abstract, universal constraints. Virtue thus acquires an instrumental character as an aspect of the art or skill of attaining one's private ends, recalling the Sophist reduction of *aretē* to *technē*. For Aristotle, conversely, ethics is devoted to an analysis of the virtues which specify our ideal finality (*eudaimonia*). Intended to "achieve and preserve the good of the community" and so promote "the humanly good," the moral virtues have as their natural harmonic the ideal fruition of the common good in the formation of the just *polis*, the *koinonía téleios* (Aristotle *Nicomachean Ethics* (1094a22-b12). To abide only by the strict personal obligations of distributive justice would not fulfill the demands of *ethics* in that higher sense in which Aristotle understood the term. Arguing that "while it is desirable to secure what is good in the case of an individual, to do so in the case of a people or a state is something finer and more sublime," Aristotle presupposes that the community possesses a reality in its own right, distinct from that of the sum of individuals (Aristotle *Nicomachean Ethics* 1094a22–b12). The ancients and medieval Scholastics expressed this in the concept of *nature* and of a "natural society" in which the *bonum commune* is specifically distinct from the composite of *bona individualia*. The virtuous life, that is, unfolds against the backdrop of the *polis;* it is here its gestures are charged with significance and derive their characteristic form and force. The life of virtue thus presupposes the *polis* even as the end of the *polis* is the perfection of the citizen *(polites)* through education and training in virtue. For Thomas Aquinas, a faithful disciple of Aristotle in this respect, moral perfection presumes the "communitas perfecta," as "the common good is the end of each individual member of the community." The "ultimate good" is at once a "common good," and indeed, in the theological teleology of Thomas, God is par excellence the "bonum commune."[6]

In addition to signifying the "particular virtue" of distributive or rectificatory justice, justice is also regarded generally by Aristotle as "complete virtue in the fullest sense" precisely as it "tends to produce or conserve the happiness (and the constituents of the happiness) of a political association" (Aristotle *Nicomachean Ethics* 1129b6–1130b8). Similarly, for Thomas, general justice or "justitia legalis" is ceded primacy over all the moral virtues inasmuch as it directs them to the "common good" which "transcends the individual good of one person" (Thomas *Summa Theologiae* 2.2, ques. 58, art. 6, 12). The subordination of social ethics to private morality, so characteristic of our modern sensibility, would thus seem an inversion of the proper order in which justice is the "sovereign virtue," and not merely an adventitious harmony of rights or interests.

In the face of the totalitarian ideologies of this century which ruthlessly subject the person to the state, such views might seem portentous. Yet the apotheosis of the state, of recent origin, differs from the primacy of the common good defended by Aristotle and Thomas. The common good was conceived distributively, as a good in which all share singly, not en masse — a good "flowing back" upon its constitutive members. As such, it reflects a distinctive conception of society as, in Maritain's words, "a whole composed of wholes"— neither an artifice of interest occasioned by contract, nor a suprapersonal "total organism" which comes to prominence in German Romanticism.[7] Herein lies, *a limine*, an insurmountable distinction from all totalitarian ideologies. Yet there are others: the transcendence of the social whole implies that a "closed society" allegedly justified on historical grounds can never suffice from the ethical point of view. The state, which aims at socioethical ideals that lie essentially beyond itself in the fruition of the common good, cannot be regarded as an Archimedean point of political reflection. Already conceived analogically by Thomas, the "communitas perfecta" must now embrace the global community forged by the intensive economic and cultural communications of our own day.

II. FROM THE SOCIAL TO THE INDIVIDUAL CONCEPTION OF NATURE

The elusive idea of nature has traditionally been the central concept in a theory of social ethics. Arising from the prephilosophic conception of "the right way," the earliest understanding of nature reflects the "first things" and "the essential character of a thing."[8]

Archelaus, the disciple of Anaxagoras and teacher of Socrates, appears to have been the first to have voiced the belief that "what is just and what is base depends not upon nature but upon convention," a view which was to become the common currency of the Sophists. In his account of Protagoras' "Of the Ancient Order of Things," Plato recalls the Sophist myth of society as a mere assemblage of individuals in whose gathering for self-preservation is the customary origin of law and justice. Opposing the conventionalist sophistry of Thrysamachus in the *Republic*, Plato rejects such a view, arguing that nature serves as the characteristic norm of personal and civic life. The specifically human is not "given" in the sense of "merely present at hand," but discovered as the unity concealed behind the manifold of appearances. Similarly, Plato insists upon the *social* quality of nature so normatively construed, for only in the whole of society can what is characteristically human be discovered and flourish. Although many have objected to the "totalitarian" quality of Plato's state, the fact that the social whole surpasses the closed political community is frequently overlooked. All through the *Republic*, Plato clearly distinguishes the phenomenal city from the ideal one. "The city of the *Republic* is the best city, the city according to nature."[9] The actual *polis* is a perishable realization, born and bound to die. Beyond it, Plato refers to human society as a whole, a microcosm of the eternal laws.

Although he developed an empirical science of politics, Aristotle never severed political nature from the normative ideal. Since the good life requires a good state, ethical ideals continue to inform politics so that individual behavior is measured by the canons of civic virtue. The legislator's primary duty consists in creating the conditions for leading a virtuous life, a life in which the citizens can develop their physical and spiritual powers in proportion and harmony. Because of the imperfection of many states, however, the good person may not in all cases coincide with the good citizen. With Aristotle, the natural quality of the state emphatically implies the *ideal* character of the concept of nature. "Natural" is not what comes first, nor what requires little effort, but rather what specifically constitutes the ideal finality of the *polis* as a *koinonía téleios:* the reign of justice and the realization of the common good.

While each of the distinctive strands of nature's signification is present in Aristotle's definition, his originality lies in so finely interweaving them that only thus does the image of the "humanly good" emerge. Since much of the history of modern moral thought may be seen as an unraveling of this conception, a few words might be offered in Aristotle's behalf. As Ernest Barker observes, the Aristotelian conception of nature signifies at once the "potentiality of development" immanent in one's primordial constitution, a growth of this potentiality "in which (one's) 'art', or creative mind has cooperated," and finally, the ideal fruition of this development as one's final cause or purpose.[10] The idea of nature reflects the biological metaphor of "bringing forth" as a principle of spontaneous motion, informed by a characteristic *telos*. As the self-illumination of "nature," the "natural law" expresses this vital dynamism and, although preceding positive legislative enactment, bears no less the mark of mind.

For Aristotle, there is no question of inferring an illicit "ought" from merely descriptive premises, for the *eudaimon* is not a bare *res cogitans*, conceived in Kantian abstraction from all purposes. The subsequent straitening of moral discourse into "descriptive" and "prescriptive" locutions fails to capture the rich texture of Aristotle's notion of "reasoned speech" which serves to indicate "what is right and what is wrong" (Aristotle *Politics* 1.2). For Aristotle has not committed the naturalistic fallacy of deriving prescriptive conclusions from merely descriptive premises through some feat of conceptual legerdemain.[11] Descriptions of virtuous action are fully explicated only if they show forth virtuous intention, that is, one's "knowledge of the good for oneself." "What I do" thus discloses virtue as an excellence to be achieved, our *areté*.

Forming the bedrock of justification, "what is good" is not derived from an angelic point of view but reflects the heritage of a linguistic community in which reason might be likened, in Barker's words, to "a 'bank and capital of the ages,' which grows by a gradual process of *social* accumulation and transmission."[12] One discerns here the delicate "aesthetic" balance of ethics (*Sittlichkeit*) and moral obligation (*Moralität*) as the "individual whole" of the moral agent presupposes the common good of the "social whole" "flowing back," in Maritain's words, upon its constitutive members.[13] *Phronesis* ("prudence") implies *sunesis*, a common apperception of the good mediated in *paideia*, and is thus irreducible to the modern conception of prudence as enlightened self-interest.[14] Such is the province of ethics for Aristotle that it unites the Apollonian ideals of "self-knowledge" and virtue so that "what I do" is reflectively disclosed in the "reasoned speech" of the perfect community (*koinonía téleios*).

With the demise of the *polis*, the complex interplay of nature (*physis*) and custom (*nomos*) would be transformed in the rationalistic tenor of Stoic thought into a concern for timeless, invariant principles—"quod semper, quod ubique." Yet despite the increasing "depoliticization" of ethics in the wake of the Hellenistic and the Roman empires, the understanding of nature retained its social implications and continued to assert the "common good" as being irreducible to the sum of individual goods. For the Stoics who believed that the "polity of mankind" was naturally ruled by Reason, the idea of a universal law (*koinòs nómos*) corresponded to the universal whole — as literally a "common pasture" (*koinòs nómos*) upon which all might safely graze.[15]

The *sacra doctrina* of the Scholastics found its natural complement in the *ratio scripta* of natural law, proceeding alike from the *lex aeterna* of the divine mind. To live as persons in community remains our ethical purpose, even though the common good of the perfect community is not an absolute good, for the entire "natural" order is subordinate to a higher, supernatural order. Has one here the intimations of the later decline of the social as the natural, ideal order? Certainly the danger implicated in the tension between two separate orders, of which the higher could simply overrule existing social structures in favor of an individual's salvation, is clear. The advent of the Reformers brought with it no lessening of this tension. As Ernst Troeltsch remarks, the distinction in Catholicism "between the lower stage of development of relative natural law and the genuinely Christian higher stage of development has (for Luther) been transferred to the individual" as the contrast between the "secular morality" of office and the personal "morality of grace."[16]

Other elements contributed to the decline of ethics as a formal discipline. The end of the Middle Ages saw the intensification of the conflict between the Supreme Pontiff and the secular princes, especially the German emperor and the kings of France. At the same time, the nominalist controversy gradually devalued the concept of nature in favor of an almighty and inscrutable divine will. While the former resulted in the assertion of the absolute supremacy of the secular sovereign, the latter's emphasis upon the divinely appointed "nature" of things led to the Reformers' belief that, with respect to the intramundane order, the proper attitude "is not one of explanation and ethical acceptance, but of religious obedience and humble submission."[17]

These distinct tendencies were united in the sixteenth century with the rise of the national states. A new theory of nature emerged that was less social in import, viewing society as a voluntary rather than a natural association. The absolute authority of the sovereign as articulated in the theory of divine right rested upon a *positive* and ultimately arbitrary decree, not upon the intrinsic rationality of the social order. The *ultima lex* was the promulgative act of the sovereign even as, in the religious realm, it was the positive, even more mysterious will of God. Even those who resisted these absolutist theories (Calvinists in England and France, the "League" in France) in the name of innate, "natural" rights conceived these in individual rather than social terms. The natural law theory that developed from these antiabsolutist, antipositivist tendencies would in fact seal the fate of the social tradition of ethics and, in the end, would discredit the very concept of a natural law.

Yet before the idea of nature lost its social character entirely, one final attempt was made to restore it. Suarez combined the traditional idea of nature as a *social* norm of law with the modern theory of law as located in the will of the legislator. The judgment that informs the legislative will follows the rule of rational nature, even though the will alone converts that rule into *law*. Thus Suarez wends his way between the Scylla of Vasquez's legal rationalism, in which law is grounded in reason, and the Charybdis of Ockham's voluntarism, in which law depends exclusively upon the sovereign will. He continues to ground the essential social structures in human nature while according their concrete realization to positive legislation. In this he succeeded in uniting, albeit briefly, the two theories of authority that so acutely divided the beginning of the modern epoch: one that originates "below" in the "natural" human community itself; the other, "from above," to which the divine right theory gave extreme expression.

The modern age did not accept Suarez's theory, much as it was influenced by it. Indeed, as the social realm came to be viewed as the outcome of individual decisions, the very idea of a social ethic became increasingly otiose. Hobbes's state of nature is in essence *antisocial*. In his mechanistic elementarism the term *nature* came to mean the very opposite of what it had signified in the classical and Scholastic traditions. While in the contemplative *eudaimonia* of Aristotle, the "felicity of this life consisteth ... in the repose of a mind satisfied," it is precisely the want of this which impresses Hobbes: "For there is no such '*finis ultimus*' nor '*summum bonum*'. ... Felicity is the continual progress of the desire, from one object to another; the attaining of the former, being still but the way to the latter."[18] The *cor inquietum*, deprived of its divine *telos*, inspires a philosophy of unease in which the natural contours of society have been reduced to a universal scramble. Thus the origin of the "state of nature" which "is called war; and such a war, as is of every man against every man," history being an inglorious "tract of time wherein the will to contend by battle is sufficiently known." It would be erroneous, however, to attribute Hobbes's individualism entirely to his materialism, for his is not even a consistent hedonistic theory of the good: not contentment, but the rational certainty of a secured future is the spur to human endeavor. The "perpetual and restless desire of power after power" which this entails creates a continuous possibility of conflict, a permanent state of war, but also the necessity to overcome it by some form of social compact.[19]

Ironically, it is not the universal harmony of agencies depicted in the *polis*, but their natural disharmony, which gives rise to society. No longer can one speak of the *natural* perfection of the social whole. For, writes Sheldon Wolin, the absolute right to all things which had been the source of chaos was, nevertheless, a part of man's nature, but one which threatened to annihilate his existence. Hence while the establishment of civil society not only contradicted man's right, and therefore his nature, it stood as the only condition which did not contradict his existence."[20] Yet of all the political thinkers of the seventeenth century, Hobbes perhaps most closely approaches the idea of society originating of necessity rather than gentlemanly accord. The only one who resembles him in this respect is Rousseau, though it is still the logical primacy of the individual which prevails. And while the Roman conception of the *sensus communis* as the seat of social sympathy recurs with Vico and Shaftesbury, it is the radical individualism, rather than the necessity of society, which social theory reflects as it develops toward contractualism.

III. ETHICS AND STRUCTURES: SOCIAL CONTRACT THEORIES AND THE SOCIOECONOMIC IMPLICATIONS OF THE ECLIPSE OF THE COMMON GOOD

From an ethical viewpoint, the most significant change in the modern conception of society consisted in the transformation of the theory of natural law into one of natural rights. The transition is a gradual one, and the idea of natural right at first appears to be no more than a logical elaboration of natural law. In describing the "state of nature" as a peaceable kingdom whose members are motivated by desire for individual happiness, and endowed with the (natural) right to pursue it, Locke invokes the authority of "the judicious Hooker." Yet nothing could be more misleading. For while Hooker's theory of natural law barely differed from Aquinas', deferring to the medieval Schoolman rather than to more recent Catholic theories, Locke's "community of nature" bore a distinctively individualistic stamp. The nature he described was that of the individual qua individual; the right, no more than a conclusion derived from the ultimacy of that right; and political society, an instrument for the exercise of that right in the preservation of life, liberty, and estate.

Resting upon a purely abstract, socially decontextualized conception of human nature, the Lockean doctrine of natural rights does not entirely belie its Whiggish inspiration. *Property* functions as the regnant metaphor for right which, with our emergence from the state of nature, becomes increasingly convertible with interest. It comes as little surprise, then, that the utilitarians would question the moral relevance of the distinction of innate, natural rights and merely acquired interests. The idea of natural right seemed no less adventitious than the interests it protected — a legal fiction dismissed by Bentham as "rhetorical nonsense,— nonsense upon stilts."[21]

Hume and Burke perceived the theoretical weakness of the idea of natural rights, as well as its ominous revolutionary potential. Indeed, the appeal to innate rights often served as a *cri de coeur* to rally support against the political status quo. Yet even so, the currency of rights was not immediately redeemable in the political arena, as witnessed in the curious shift of Paine's argument in his *Rights of Man:* the idea of rights as a legal abstraction is defended in the first part, only to yield in the second to his invocation of the principle of utility. The primitive society, he now argues, is not the "state of nature" with its attendant rights, but rather the economic society founded on the principle of exchange which, according to Adam Smith, simply represented the "natural" harmony of interests.

Philosophy, of course, bears ample testimony that the usefulness of an idea is seldom limited by its logically rigorous use. The new doctrine of individual, abstract rights, as expressed in the idea of a "social contract," was thus designed to play a significant justificatory role for the modern nation-state. The objection, first enunciated by Hume, and repeated by Smith, Paley, and Bentham, that no historical evidence supports the hypothesis of an original contract, fails to address what is novel in the theory. As was suggested by several of its proponents, the issue is not one of *quid facti* but of *quid juris*. For Kant, such a contract is "by no means to be necessarily assumed to be a fact—indeed, it is not even possible as such"; it is rather "a mere idea of reason which has, however, its undoubted (practical) reality" as "the touchstone of the legitimacy of every public enactment."[22] A similar argument has gained renewed currency in the writings of John Rawls.

Contract, then, serves as an ideal, symbolic expression of the conditions of legitimate representation, describing, in Kant's words, "the act by means of which the people constitute themselves a state," or "more properly," the "Idea of that act that alone enables us to conceive of the legitimacy of the state. According to the original contract, all (*omnes et singuli*) the people give up their external freedom in order to take it back again immediately as members of a commonwealth, that is, the people regarded as the state (*universi*)."[23] Novel in contractual theory is the supposition that the "common entity" thereby composed is not the "natural" expression of the common good, but rather a supreme artifice occasioned for the representation of individual interests and rights.

A certain discrepancy is thus apparent between the formal, symbolic role of social contract in the self-illumination of society and its explicit, individualistic content. For while such symbolization is predicated upon the *essentially* social character of existence—one's natural participation in the *xynon*, the common, as Heraclitus called it—the Lockean contract is finally little more than adventitious in origin.[24] Not only is the domain of rights envisioned as logically prior to the articulation of society per se; but with the "emancipation of . . . productive acquisitiveness" which is itself "accidentally beneficent" the social caveats operative in the state of nature are superseded.[25] And though a certain civility of mores is presumed in Locke's state of nature, there is no natural necessity impelling one to live in society.

Yet if society is construed as the grand issue of convention, Socrates' criticism of the Sophists seems entirely apropos, for what elusive alchemy could endow the economy of interest with the lawlike character of right? The supposition of rights antecedent to the conception of society is indeed, as Ernest Barker notes, a *contradictio in adjecto*, "the difficulty of such a prepolitical condition (being) that it is really political. Locke's state of nature, with its regime of recognized rights, is already a political society."[26]

Rousseau denies that the social bond (*lien social*) issues from a sense of social sympathy, differing in this respect from Diderot, Grotius, and the Encyclopedists.[27] Yet while for Locke, sovereignty is resolved into the "natural rights" of the contractors, for Rousseau, the generation of the sovereign *volonté générale* assumes a privileged moral status in its own right. Although logically prior to the formation of the social contract, the individual attains full moral stature only through it; thus, "man acquires with civil society, moral freedom, which alone makes man the master of himself."[28] So accounting for the genesis of sovereignty, Rousseau departs from Hobbes's assumption that it is antithetical to freedom. Sovereignty arises not through a *pactum subjectionis*, but a "reciprocal commitment between society and the individual so that each person, in making a contract, as it were, with himself, finds himself doubly committed, first as a member of the state in relation to the sovereign."[29] The sovereignty of the general will implies, then, not the abrogation of freedom, but its autonomous exercise, for "to be governed by appetite alone is slavery, while obedience to a law one prescribes to oneself is freedom."[30]

Yet though one is wholly subject, one is not wholly sovereign, and therein lies the rub. For Rousseau expressly states that the will of all (*omnes et universi*) is not reducible without remainder to the unity of individual wills in "gratuitous combination" (*omnes ut singuli*) — in which case the unity of wills, being resolvable into the will of each, would be "a mere rational entity." On the contrary, the general will enjoys such moral precedence that "in order that the social pact be not an empty formula, it is tacitly implied in that commitment — which *alone* can give force to all others — that whoever refuses to obey the general will shall be constrained to do so by the whole body, which means nothing other than that he shall be forced to be free."[31] It is thus that the "extravagant shepherd" justifies the generation of political authority, at once harking back to the innate rights of the individual championed by Locke, and anticipating "the new style of German thought which was to divinize the Folk-person" in its historicization of law "as the expression in time of the general will or consciousness of right which proceeds from that person."[32]

Rousseau's remarkable status as a Janus-like figure in the history of natural law lies in his assumption that sovereignty is inalienable while the proper subject of sovereignty is not the aggregate of individual wills but the constituted unity or *persona moralis* of the state. He contends: "Whoever ventures on the enterprise of setting up a people must be ready, shall we say, to change human nature, to transform each individual, who by himself is entirely complete and solitary, into a part of a much greater whole, from which that same individual will then receive, in a sense, his life and his being."[33] Moral freedom, as such, is not the *condition* of contract but its *consequence* as the sovereign artificer is defined.

The state is established not through a natural harmony of feelings but through "unifying acts of the will and directing them to a common goal."[34] The state, although itself of voluntaristic construction, thus fulfills the formal, symbolic role of social incorporation as an "artificial body" which, in the "act of association ... acquires its unity, its common ego, its life and its will."[35] The "indivisible" sovereignty so generated rests in the hypostasis of a general will which unifies in itself the manifold of individual wills as parts of "a much greater whole." The "universal voice" of law, in *Emile* ascribed to the individual conscience conformed to natural law, is metamorphosed into the sovereign fiat of the general will. One has the consummate irony that in Rousseau's very dispute with Hobbes, one is coerced to be free: ethics remains the language of *Leviathan*.

In our own time, this concentration of authority in one social body has resulted in serious political crises, both by sapping social life of the vital strength which it can find only in the so-called intermediate bodies, and by constantly obstructing much-needed international agreements requiring the acknowledgment of sovereignty beyond that of the state. Although both problems flow directly from the lack of a sound basis for the social structure, most attempts made to remedy them have neglected the underlying causes.

The decline of the intermediate bodies in favor of an unlimited state power, and the concomitant loss of their autonomy, began with the self-proclaimed absolutism of the modern national state. From the onset, a powerful bureaucracy attempted, usually with success, to deprive the guilds and corporations of their authority. Only where that political authority itself remained tenuous, such as in the German Empire, did the lower social bodies retain some independence. German theoreticians, especially Nettelbladt, applied the same doctrine of natural right upon which the state is based to all associations as being within their own sphere equally endowed with social autonomy. In strongly organized national states, especially France, however, the trend was to deprive these bodies of all independent power and to derive their authority entirely from the state.

Rousseau's social theory, although opposed to absolute authority in the political ruler, nevertheless found no place for such free associations, recognizing only the political society in his social contract — indeed, the idea of a *political* contract is altogether lacking. Even Hegel, the first thinker of the modern age to attempt a genuine social ethics, failed to provide an adequate framework. In restoring the relative social independence of the intermediate associations, he felt it necessary to subordinate them to the state, thus intensifying the problem of establishing an international authority. Hegel's "strong" theory of the state and Marx's even stronger assertion of the primacy of the stateless society culminated in the reassertion of the "common good" in Continental philosophy, though, with the absorption of the power of autonomous or semi-autonomous social bodies (in Marx) and the relative subordination of the individual, its meaning has changed considerably.

At its origin, the economic upsurge of the modern age was wholly state-directed. Yet with the decline of the mercantilist system, beginning with the Physiocrats, the economic sphere became more and more a private domain only reluctantly tolerating political intervention. Admittedly, economic activity has always been social in nature, never more so than in the intense cooperation of the modern age. The classical economists were well aware of this, although the natural identity assumed between public and private interests led to an individualistic construal of labor. Hence, the clearly social division of labor which lies at the root of Smith's theory is based upon the *individual*'s desire to "truck, barter, and exchange" rather than upon the social nature of all fully human activity. Exchange becomes a means for more effectively advancing one's private interests, "the freedom of conscience in trade."[36]

The production process resolves itself into the activity of individuals organized into social cooperation for the pursuit of private satisfaction. The ultimate end, profit, retains its supremely individualistic character, even in a cooperative system: "It is not from the benevolence of the butcher, the brewer, or the baker," writes Smith, "that we expect our dinner, but from their regard to their own interest. We address ourselves, not to their humanity but to their self-love, and never talk to them of our own necessities — but of their advantages."[37] So the easy commerce of "private vice" and "public virtue" lauded by Mandeville serves to reconcile the highly socialized methods of modern economies with the strictly private purposes they promote. Marx called this one of the "contradictions" of the capitalist system. Yet it is neither a contradiction nor an exclusively capitalist phenomenon. Indeed, in his later writings, Marx himself appears to share the "instrumentalist" assumptions of the classical economists, positing the primacy of economic production. Productive relations thus precede other social and cultural relations and are themselves determined by the historical *forces* of production:

> The social relations within which individuals produce, the social relations of production, are altered, transformed, with the change and development of the material means of production, of the forces of production. The relations of production in their totality constitute what is called the social relations, society, and moreover, a society at a definite stage of historic development. . . .[38]

If Marx has turned Hegel on his head, one would perhaps wish him righted a bit. For Marx's earlier writings, testifying to the influence of Fichte and Hegel, emphasize human creativity as manifest in, yet not wholly subordinate to, economic activity. All too frequently in its relatively short history, economics has been regarded as a realm of unchangeable laws, an aspect of physical anthropology, or a domain of strictly private behavior organized in self-chosen forms of cooperation. Save for its technical aspects, the intrinsically social and cultural character of this activity has seldom been fully acknowledged. Due to a general failure to recognize the intrinsically social quality of economic activity, problems of distributive justice have often been treated as pertaining to the individual responsibility of employers, managers, and workers — a matter of duties effective *within* an existing system. Little attention, however, has been devoted to the conception of alternative social models, ideal structures of cooperation as the substantive *ethical* expression of the common good.

The political supremacy of the state, reflected in the subsumption of intermediate social bodies and the emancipation of the economic sphere, has been of no less consequence for international relations. For modern political thought has failed in a signal fashion to develop social structures that would effectively mediate the conflict of national interests. Almost from its inception, the modern philosophy of international law has assumed without question the absolute sovereignty of the state. International law has, of course, a long and complex history, beginning with the role of the *jus gentium* in Roman jurisprudence. Despite the Stoic embellishments of the *Corpus Juris Civilis*, the *jus gentium* consisted essentially in the commercial law pertaining to the dealings of Romans with others. By its greater universality, it surpassed local municipal laws and customs and could thus provide a common foundation for positive legislation. The issue of sovereignty was hardly in dispute and the relations among nations per se received little attention.

The cosmopolitan character of the *jus gentium* represented the common quality which positive laws and customs were assumed to possess among all peoples. Only with Vitoria and Suarez does the law of nations become a more or less coherent set of principles (conformed to the natural law) for the regulation of international relations. While Vitoria dealt with the specific issue of Spain's relations with its American colonies, Suarez developed a more universal perspective based upon the idea of the entire human race as moral community:

> The human race, howsoever divided into various peoples and kingdoms, always has a certain unity, not only specific, but also as it were political and moral. . . . Therefore although

each perfect city, state, or kingdom constitutes in itself a perfect community consisting of its own members, nevertheless each of them is also a member in a certain fashion of this universe, so far as it concerns the human race. . . . For this reason therefore they have need of some law, by which they may be directed and rightly ordered in this kind of communication and society.[39]

Contending that "the precepts of the law of nations differ from the precepts of the civil law in the fact that they consist not in something written, but in customs—of all or almost all nations," Suarez assumes that the *jus gentium* is at once customary in origin yet consistent with the natural law.[40] He thereby synthesizes the "positive," customary aspect of the law of nations with its rational, a priori character. Significantly, this rational apriority is legitimated not by the needs or interests of individual nations, but rather by the community of the human race itself. When in subsequent years either the apriority or the social quality of this apriority was lost, attempts to establish a system of international law became increasingly problematic and resulted mostly in limited agreements for the mutual benefits of a few nations.

Yet can the national state in the modern world still be regarded as the "perfect" society? Surely the state has lost the self-sufficiency upon which its earlier absolute sovereignty was founded —a loss apparent in the political as well as in the economic sphere. The idea of a world economy which has guided economists since the eighteenth century has in our day become a reality. Indeed, the commerce of nations is such that few would be able to sustain a civilized level of existence if international economic exchange were to collapse. The emergence of two ideologically opposed world powers, either capable of destroying the other, has led to the de facto political interdependence of the developed nations; while the modern era has witnessed an even greater economic dependence on the part of the erstwhile colonies. Unprecedented as it is, this interdependence suggests that the traditional conception of national sovereignty is a theoretical *cul de sac* which can no longer serve as a valid perspective for assessing the behavior of states. Autarchy is hardly an imaginable political ideal, and the need for a greater degree of international cooperation is generally recognized. Yet the prospect of even a limited supranational sovereignty appears as remote today as when Grotius first surveyed the emergent states.

In 1920, commenting on the economy of interests and the eclipse of the common good, R. H. Tawney wrote in *The Acquisitive Society:*

> To say that the end of social institutions is happiness, is to say that they have no common end at all. For happiness is individual, and to make happiness the object of society is to resolve society itself into the ambitions of numberless individuals, each directed toward the attainment of some personal purpose.[41]

Happiness is evanescent, the promise unfulfilled, and, as in Auden's words at the eve of the Second World War, we shudder "lest we should see where we are, / Lost in a haunted wood, / Children afraid of the night / Who have never been happy or good." Still then, as now, the script is not despair, and though "our world in stupor lies," it may yet "show an affirming flame."[42]

NOTES

1. Wallace Stevens, "The Poems of Our Climate," in *The Palm at the End of the Mind* (New York: Random House, 1967), p. 158.

2. Niccolò Machiavelli, *The Prince and The Discourses*, trans. Luigi Ricci, rev. E. R. P. Vincent (New York: Random House, 1940), pp. 64–65.

3. Benedetto Croce, *Elementi di politica*, p. 60, as quoted in Isaiah Berlin, "The Originality of Machiavelli," in *Against the Current*, ed. Henry Hardy (New York: Viking Press, 1980), p. 53.

4. Thomas Nagel, "Ruthlessness in Public Life," in *Public and Private Morality*, ed. Stuart Hampshire (Cambridge: At the University Press, 1978), p. 78.

5. Hampshire, *Public and Private Morality*, p. ix.

6. Thomas *Summa Theologiae* 2-3, ques. 58, art. 7, 9; 1–2, ques. 90, art. 2. Our treatment of Thomas is indebted to I. T. Eschmann, "In Defense of Jacques Maritain," *The Modern Schoolman* 22, no. 4 (May 1945): 183–208.

7. Jacques Maritain, "The Person and the Common Good," in *The Social and Political Philosophy of Jacques Maritain*, ed. Joseph W.

Evans and Leo R. Ward (New York: Charles Scribner's Sons, 1955), pp. 320-21.

8. Leo Strauss, *Natural Right and History* (Chicago: University of Chicago Press, 1950), pp. 82-83.

9. Ibid., p. 119.

10. Ernest Barker, "Translator's Introduction" to Otto Gierke, *Natural Law and the Theory of Society* (Cambridge: At the University Press, 1958), p. xxxv. Cf. Alasdair MacIntyre's contention that classical Aristotelian ethics "presupposes some account of potentiality and act, some account of the essence of man as a rational animal and above all some account of the human *telos*. . . . We thus have a threefold scheme in which human-nature-as-it-happens-to-be (human nature in its untutored state) is initially discrepant and discordant with the precepts of ethics and needs to be transformed by the instruction of practical reason and experience into human-nature-as-it-could-be-if-it-realized-its-*telos*. Each of the three elements of the scheme — the conception of untutored human nature, the conception of the precepts of rational ethics and the conception of human-nature-as-it-could-be-if-it-realized-its-*telos* — requires reference to the other two if its status and function are to be intelligible" (Alasdair MacIntyre, *After Virtue* [Notre Dame, Ind.: University of Notre Dame Press, 1981, 1984], pp. 52-53).

11. See Bernard Williams' perceptive analysis in *Ethics and the Limits of Philosophy* (Cambridge, Mass.: Harvard University Press, 1958), pp. 51f., 121f.

12. Barker, "Translator's Introduction" to Gierke, *Natural Law and the Theory of Society*, p. xlix.

13. Maritain, "The Person and the Common Good," p. 87.

14. Cf. Hans-Georg Gadamer, *Truth and Method*, 2nd ed. (New York: Crossroad Publishing Co., 1965), pp. 278f.; and *The Idea of the Good in Platonic-Aristotelian Philosophy*, trans. P. Christopher Smith (New Haven, Conn.: Yale University Press, 1986), pp. 159f.

15. Barker, "Translator's Introduction" to Gierke, *Natural Law and the Theory of Society*, pp. xxxvi, xxxviii–xl.

16. Ernst Troeltsch, *The Social Teaching of the Christian Churches*, trans. Olive Wyon, vol. 2 (Chicago: University of Chicago Press, 1931), p. 508.

17. Ibid., p. 503.

18. Thomas Hobbes, *Leviathan*, in *British Moralists 1650–1800*, vol. 1, ed. D. D. Raphael (Oxford: Clarendon Press, 1969), p. 32, no. 44.

19. Ibid., p. 36, no. 50; pp. 32-33, no. 44.

20. Sheldon Wolin, *Politics and Vision* (Boston: Little, Brown & Co., 1960), p. 263.

21. Jeremy Bentham, *Anarchical Fallacies*, in *The Works of Jeremy Bentham*, ed. J. Bowring (Edinburgh, 1943), 2:523.

22. Immanuel Kant *Werke* 6.380f., as quoted in Ernst Cassirer, *Rousseau, Kant, Goethe: Two Essays*, trans. James Gutmann, Paul Oskar Kristeller, and John Herman Randall, Jr. (Hamden, Conn.: Archon Books, 1961), p. 35.

23. Immanuel Kant *Rechtslehre*, par. 47 (*Werke* 7.122), *The Metaphysical Elements of Justice*, trans. John Ladd (Indianapolis: Bobbs-Merrill Co., 1965), pp. 80f.

24. Cf. Eric Voegelin, *The New Science of Politics* (Chicago: University of Chicago Press, 1952), pp. 27–28.

25. Strauss, *Natural Right and History*, p. 248.

26. Ernest Barker, *Social Contract: Essays by Locke, Hume, and Rousseau* (London: Oxford University Press, 1947), p. xx.

27. Cf. Cassirer, *Rousseau, Kant, Goethe*, pp. 27–28.

28. Jean-Jacques Rousseau, *The Social Contract*, trans. Maurice Cranston (New York: Penguin Books, 1968), p. 65.

29. Ibid., p. 62.

30. Ibid., p. 65.

31. Ibid., p. 64.

32. Barker, *Social Contract*, p. xxx; see also pp. xxxiv–xxxv.

33. Rousseau, *The Social Contract*, p. 84.

34. Cassirer, *Rousseau, Kant, Goethe*, p. 30.

35. Rousseau, *The Social Contract*, p. 61.

36. Morellet, as quoted in Wolin, *Politics and Vision*, p. 340.

37. Adam Smith, *The Wealth of Nations* (Chicago: University of Chicago Press, 1976), pp. 17–18.

38. Karl Marx *Werke* 6.408 (*Selected Works*, 1:91).

39. Francisco Suarez, *De Legibus*, chap. 19, in *Selections from Three Works*, ed. James Scott (Oxford: Clarendon Press, 1944), pp. 348–49.

40. Ibid., p. 345.

41. R. H. Tawney, *The Acquisitive Society* (New York: Harcourt, Brace, & World, 1920), p. 29.

42. W. H. Auden, "September 1, 1939."

10
Evading the Shadows: Freedom and the Social World
RUTH L. SMITH

IN THE CONTINUING ATTEMPT to explore the historical construction of liberalism and to deconstruct its formal and naturalistic claims, the relationship between freedom and the social world has been variously reconceived. Concepts of intersubjectivity and relationality, concepts of the common good, and concepts of difference, while distinct from each other, are all ways of dislodging the imperial claims of the autonomous self as the seat of freedom and introducing new questions about the meaning and construction of the social world.[1] This paper is a continuation of this project in its exploration of strands of liberal thought that merge in the attribution of "otherness" to those persons and aspects of life outside the autonomous, free, and universal self. In this convergence, ways in which the social world lies in the shadow of freedom emerge: in the definition of society as a contingent and, therefore, lesser life form; in the attribution of otherness to those persons outside the dominant construction of the self as autonomous; and in the hegemonic aspects of social and moral theories that systematically exclude the social and moral worlds of those defined as "other."

The problem of the self and otherness has many aspects. I am concerned with the otherness historically created through the construction of a self that in its universal requirements enacts exclusion by displacing into the realm of the contingent and dependent all that is unlike it and all that threatens its autonomy. In this displacement, autonomy removes all otherness from itself and claims all freedom for itself; the "unfree" is the other and the other is "unfree." This liberal resolution of the self and other relationship evades two problems. One, contingency is disarmed and need not be confronted or taken into the self. Two, those persons who are seen to be more contingent, more socially embedded, and less free, are through the attribution of otherness delegitimated as sources of social and moral power.

I explore the problem of those who are historically "other" in relation to the idea that society is other, an intertwining whose modern liberal form begins to take shape in the Reformation.[2] My argument is that in the connection between our notions of who is other and of society, society becomes the other, at least in part, by virtue of who gets to be free and who has to be in the social world, by virtue of who can evade their otherness and who carries the otherness for those who are "free." This problem is reproduced in moral and social theories that privilege the bourgeois self and so reiterate notions of who is other through implicit and explicit statements that not all persons or worlds count as legitimate sources for social and moral reflection. In the failure to recognize their own contingency in the practices of theory, the makers of theories can themselves evade their otherness by erasing those to whom they are other. I am, then, looking at the historical construction of otherness as part of self-construction and the presence of this construction in theory making.

My approach is one of analysis and contemplation; I want both to argue and to understand. Even to respond to this problem is difficult in ways that we do not readily perceive, ways inherited from the liberal emphasis on autonomy, from the Christian emphasis on universality, and from the Western emphasis on permanence. These strands all speak in unison in their statement that if the world belongs to all, the all are those who are not "other" and who can remain untouched by otherness. Even when the practitioners of theory are those who are historically the other—for example, women—we may reproduce the hegemony by which our terms of freedom and participation assert our dominance, our lack of contingency, and render others mute. Maria C. Lugones and Elizabeth V. Spelman describe this contradiction for Hispanic women confronting the theories of Anglo women. "So your being ill at ease in our worlds lacks the features of our being ill at ease in yours precisely because you can leave and you can always tell yourselves that you will be soon out of there and because the wholeness of your selves is never touched by us, we have no tendency to remake you in our image."³

To think about otherness requires that we who make theory slow down our thoughts, stretch out the race to analysis, loosen our grip on the answer, assume an attitude of humility. In dashing over our words we often become facile; we avoid the anguish they may cause us, the self-reflection they may provoke. In the ease of good vocabularies and full bellies we may design the exterior of our social and moral theories with elaborate decoration but without an interior. We also design that lack. In our urgency we have no time. As historian of religions Charles Long remarks with regard to Thomas Altizer's death-of-God theology: "He is a man who speaks of death so glibly as if he has never experienced or is afraid to experience the dying and the killing itself. He wishes for us to plunge on, or, to put it in Frederick Jackson Turner's language, to move on to a new frontier. There is no patience, no meditative attitude, no attentiveness in his proposal."⁴

Long's concern in his essay is the invisibility and concealment that, through "a language which is the expression of a hermeneutics of conquest and suppression," marks much of the analysis of black religion in America.⁵ We displace our otherness onto the others whose gaze we cannot meet by terms which appear to include but are dominating and which force inclusion by expansion instead of confronting historical contradictions. In describing the problem of otherness, Long tries to get through to us once again by recalling the words of the black writer Ralph Ellison in his novel *Invisible Man*. "Nor is my invisibility exactly a matter of a biochemical accident of my epidermis. That inevitability to which I refer occurs because of a peculiar disposition of the eyes of those with whom I come in contact. A matter of construction of the *inner eyes*, those eyes with which they look through their physical eyes upon reality."⁶

The words of Lugones and Spelman and of Long and Ellison remind us that to talk about otherness is immediately to talk about society, for these realities confirm and disguise each other. In what comes to be liberal thought, each expresses contingency and limitation in contrast to the autonomy of freedom. Each impinges on the permanence, unity, and universality that merge with autonomy in the construction of a self that is impermeable. In the construction of the inner eye of the liberal self, the social and psychological experiences of autonomy are predicated on oblivion to all that might call it into question. Those aspects of reality that express contingency and limitation, dependency and need, are externalized as both threatening and trivial.

My argument at this point is not that liberalism is necessarily wrong to find contingency and limitation problematic. My argument is with the social construction of contingency and permanence, limitation and universality, in such a way that assigns the threatening and the trivial to people who are outside the canons of autonomy in their lack of economic or political or cultural power. The aspect of threat is hidden by the liberal categories through which the independent and the derivative, the essential and the accidental, appear to be naturally divided. This division obscures the power that is required to render groups of people invisible, to externalize what is accidental and dependent. What is threatening, once removed from the self, is then trivialized. At this point those who are other and society merge. In the face of the autonomous self, what could be more trivial than to be associated with society instead of autonomy, with groups and relationships instead of freedom and self-sovereignty, with particulars instead of universals?

Indeed, in the Western tradition we have for the most part placed the contingent and the particular under suspicion to the point of denying their capacity to yield meaning at all. Both otherness and society have their meaning only as the negation of autonomy. By being nothing, they set off the presence of autonomy as the only something. As the repository of contingency and particularity, otherness and society, they are only conditions of nonfreedom and nondirection. They consist of those who impede the teleology of freedom and its career of growth. They consist of imperfections to growth, of that which requires adjustment to fit.

Contingency also reminds us of need and necessity: the necessity by which we all are born and we die; the necessity by which we all must eat, be clothed, and sheltered; the necessity that each of us carries at every moment but which becomes abstract in the marketplace as a function of exchange. This necessity of ours does not fit the world of autonomy, for it speaks of need and insufficiency and incompleteness. By making those whose needs are primary the repository of need we erase our need. We become strangers when we need because the institutions of need are strangers to liberal society, to the market. We become moral aliens when we need, for what can those who need tell those of us who are complete about morality?

Troeltsch, for all of his attention to historical events, struggles to define the significance of contingency. In the antinomy of contingency and freedom, Troeltsch follows the neo-Kantian route whereby the binary relationship is the paradigm and one side is privileged over the other.[7] The moral power of contingency lies in what the contingent evokes from the noncontingent. As Long observes of Troeltsch's analysis, if Christianity can speak for the lower classes, this is a function of its universality and not of its particularity.[8] The contingent is a stranger to truth.

We fear the contingent as that which is imperfect and insufficient. We also fear the contingent as that which is social and located. In fearing our shadow, we also fear ourselves, ourselves who are free of location and so can only be critical. We fear the death that is evaded in criticism, the assumption of perfection embedded in criticism, the nothing of criticism that stands in no place. In response, we displace fear so that it is outside autonomy, outside criticism, outside social and moral theory, outside truth.

Through bourgeois autonomy we protect ourselves from need and contingency, and by emptying those categories of meaning we protect ourselves from those whom we consign to contingency. Sartre links these problems specifically in his essay "Portrait of the Antisemite." In this essay Sartre explores his philosophical claim that we avoid freedom and authenticity because real freedom confronts us with our incompleteness, with our nothingness. The anti-Semite turns his or her own fear of freedom, and therefore of otherness, onto the Jew to whom he or she attributes only negative freedom, the freedom to do evil.[9]

The Western mistrust and devaluation of the contingent and the particular has come under fresh scrutiny in philosophies of deconstruction. According to this argument the privileging of universality and permanence is part of the commitment to the metaphysics of presence that has dominated Western thought, that is, the presumption of an all-controlling and infinitely extensive subjectivity. The terms of this presence are consolidated in the autonomous self that stands behind and speaks for all reality with a singular universal voice. Its identity is neither socially nor historically made but is the essence of an individuality that is given and lies behind all particularity.[10]

The deconstructionist makes the counterargument that the identity of selves is not given but is in the play of self-sameness and otherness or alterity. The self-other relationship is not external and accidental. That is, otherness is not added on to essential self-sameness as the unknown absence or negativity to be brought under the domination, knowledge, and ownership of the essential self. The "we" here is fluid, as is the "other." To be a self is also to be other. This perspective is not entirely recent news. If Hegel finally resolves the problem from the position of the absolute self, he also makes clear that identity is not sameness; identity always occurs with difference.[11]

Derrida pushes the resistance aspect of the Hegelian dialectic in which the otherness of each of us is differentially and "fully" intertwined with subjective self-consciousness. The experience of subjectivity does not have primacy over the experience of otherness. Each of us is an other to ourselves and to others. Otherness is as primary as self-sameness. Furthermore, otherness is absence but it is not nothing. The self and otherness are each incomplete, and each is the more. Only if the self is incomplete can it become anything. Therefore, self and other cannot be held in mutually exclusive opposition but have a "codependent" relationship at all points.[12]

To redefine the relation between self and other requires the reformulation of the notion of freedom. Freedom applies not only to the self but to that which is not the self. The freedom of the autonomous self is a freedom of exclusion and mastery. All that is not the self impinges on essential freedom and must therefore be conquered and contained. This includes all others and it includes society. The others who are excluded from power in bourgeois institutions are controlled through strategies of domination, including the domination of this notion of freedom whose exercise demands the acceptance of the terms of the bourgeois world. The perspective of deconstruction allows us to understand that those who are outside the bourgeois construction of individuality do not have to be made like us to be free. They do not have to convert to the social contract of self-interested individuality, and its counterpart of disinterest, to legitimate their activity.[13]

From this perspective on society, freedom is not the property of the autonomous self but applies to the institutions of the social world. The social world is not the other to be overcome by the self. The boundaries of the self are not divided between the subject and the social world whose attachments threaten the freedom of the self. Objectivity and subjectivity exist differentially at all points in the self and in social institutions. As Michael Ryan says in extending deconstruction in this way, "The objective institutionality of the subject . . . must also be 'liberated' if something resembling subjective freedom is to be attained."[14] To consider social relations simply as contingent and alienating aspects to be overcome sheerly by a nonalienated self perpetuates conditions of unfreedom. Feminist theorists make this point very concretely in arguing that the freedom of women requires that justice be brought to bear on the institutions and relations of the private sphere.[15]

I use the language of deconstruction to open up the problem of otherness, not to resolve or exhaust it. To imagine the self and other in deconstructed terms appears to solve the philosophical question by making difference instead of sameness the pivot of the self-other relationship. However, the move to the idea of difference can also neutralize the critical demands of the problem of otherness, or at least make them implicit instead of explicit. The trivializing of the problem of contingency in liberal thought is reproduced when the reality of self and other is constructed to be so unstable as to evade historical identity. The "we" and the "other" are not so fluid as to be without locations. If the categories of self and other are better understood differentially instead of dualistically, they still must be held accountable to the historical relationship between domination and otherness.[16]

Part of the strength of Sartre's position lies in his argument that explicitly connects otherness and domination. We create otherness through ejecting otherness from ourselves and objectifying those whom we fear, those who threaten us. In this merging of our failure to confront our own nothingness and our assignment of it to others, we inauthentically absolutize our subjectivity as the universal measure. At this point we run into trouble with Sartre's construction of the self. While he recognizes the presence of nothingness and our desire to evade it, he also retains an assumption of the autonomous self and of the nothing as outside of this "real" self. Thinkers from the deconstructionist perspective are critical of Sartre's continuation of the primacy of the subject in his view of authenticity as that which must overcome the negative other. Ryan, for example, argues that Sartre reproduces an extended subjectivity in his treatment of otherness as the negative nothing whose objectification must be overcome to obtain subjective freedom.[17]

Ryan's point is well taken; Sartre's subject is always struggling to assert subjectivity over the negation of objectivity. Further, in maintaining the primacy of the subject Sartre shifts to universal ground and the denial of difference, as when he joins anti-Semitism with all other forms of racial hatred, erasing the historical particularity of anti-Semitism itself.[18] Yet Sartre grasps something that seems to elude the deconstructionist position, that is, the force and threat and concreteness of otherness. Difference is not necessarily benign. With Sartre we cannot slide out of bad faith through deconstructing our categories; our behavior is at issue. Sartre knows that we are talking about evil, fear, and guilt not to be resolved by a philosophy that potentially can free us from digging in on ourselves. Sartre presents us with a construct that needs refiguring and with our own imperialism in our creation of otherness.

Even if we are all both self and other, so that the language of inclusion and exclusion no longer logically obtains, some of us do in fact have the power to create terms of exclusion and inclusion. Some of us do set terms for the other whom we ask to validate our theories. Our discourse is implicated in the creation of otherness when it is the only means of exchange, when we open the gates but construct a passage leading only into our property. In deconstruction, as in liberalism, through theory we make the other like us. In that process we erase the other and erase our own otherness. Even if all is "difference" it is we who have decided that this is the case. Whatever considerable significance this concept has, we should be aware that again we have converted everyone to ourselves. Lugones and Spelman speak to this problem in their article written alternatively in Hispanic and Anglo voices: "We and you do not talk the same language. When we talk we use your language: the language of your experience and of your theories. We try to use it to communicate our world of experience. But since your language and your theories are inadequate in expressing our experiences, we only succeed in communicating our experience of exclusion."[19]

A more concretely historical perspective pushes us back to examine more closely the otherness created in liberalism, to those patterns of thought and relationship that we find so habitual. We return to the problem of society as other. If otherness in liberal thought is controlled by autonomy, it is directly expressed through the notion of self-interest.[20] Society exists as the arena in which to pursue our interests and nothing more. Its meaning wobbles between two negatives. First, society is lesser than the individual who transcends it in essential freedom. As Roberto Unger argues: "Groups are artificial because all values are individual and subjective. If the group had an autonomous existence and were a source of value in its own right, we could no longer maintain that all ends were individual."[21]

Second, society is impoverished because it is tainted by that which it makes possible, the pursuit of interest and power. Society is necessary so that we will not be at each other's throats. Its contrivances never lose the coloration of self-interest. Society itself is perceived, inasmuch as it has an independent reality at all, as otherness. Its order bespeaks our own contingency. This Augustinian version of society is, as Norman O. Brown notes, greatly intensified with Luther's Reformation thought.[22] It emerges in early liberalism with Hobbes, has an ambivalent place in Locke, disappears in the more benign view of human nature that develops in the nineteenth century, and then reemerges as a voice of liberalism with thinkers such as Reinhold Niebuhr in the twentieth century. Society is the problem of order.

This version of the problem of order, however, is the domesticated one. It universalizes the problem by universalizing the market concept of self-interest. Self-interest is the liberal response to its otherness. In the market all persons are part member and part alien, part threat to one's own interests. That any one may be other makes possible the calculation of interest as a basis for social relations. It also means that all relations potentially can be jeopardized, as all are subject to the calculation of interest. In Lewis Hyde's terms, no one is protected by proximity to "tribe" or "brotherhood."[23]

The problem of valuing any form of relationship plagues liberalism, but the familiarity of its solutions keeps the plague at bay. We see these liberal solutions, for example, in Reinhold Niebuhr's notions of gregariousness and community, of the necessity of political life, of the more generous relations he locates in the private sphere.[24] All of these are residual expressions of kinds of social connection which are acknowledged but unanalyzed, as if they are natural. At the same time their construction makes them expressions of society that are correlative with autonomy. Their existence keeps self-interest from eating up the core and provides a background for individual self-expression. This construction of relations maintains the primacy not only of the individual but also of groups with market and political power. More to the point of my argument, it masks the externalization of the inner division of self and other whereby some selves order others. In what comes to be divisions of classes, races, and genders, this distinction is institutionalized so that it appears natural, obscuring not only structural oppression but also the otherness of the oppressor by associating those who "need" order because they are contingent with the contingency of the society that delivers order.

The status of social relations carries a further ambiguity. Social relations impinge on freedom and so have the negative power to block liberal transcendence. But social relations also express the universal design of the bourgeois world and so have the positive power to block the recognition of the social values in the worlds of others. Bourgeois relations are good enough in their "natural" form to transcend the value of all other previous and currently existing social worlds. Indeed, they deny that such worlds as worlds exist. However, bourgeois relations are not as good as the bourgeois individual whose transcendence involves leaving the social world behind. This transcendence is a cultural belief and also a religious one.

Its religious expression is suppressed as liberal theory becomes more secular; nonetheless, the theological formulations reinforce the negativity of society as the absence of freedom at several points. Neither groups nor societies participate in the sacred. The primary experience of the sacred takes place between the individual and God. The central religious problem, like that of the social contract, is how individuals may come together at all. This problem is resolved through a God whose universal authority and paternity relates us. In turn, by being related to this God we can establish our relationships, an idea perhaps most familiar to Americans in the Puritan covenant. Thus, society takes place only by universal imposition. Any particular expression of our spirit is not only inadequate but somehow contaminated in the misfit between essence and manifestation. As Unger says, "He will fear every social position or task as a threat to the completeness of his being."[25]

The connection between freedom and universality requires a kind of transcendence that demands an other. Lewis Hyde argues that this demand results from the Christian assertion of "universal brotherhood" which saw those outside its fold not simply as strangers but as aliens. Anyone outside the group was necessarily an enemy. "Such aggressive faith leaves a blind spot in the spirit of universal brotherhood. A covert boundary lies in the shadow that falls behind an unbounded compassion and much that unfolds during the Middle Ages, from anti-Semitism to the Church's spiritual imperialism, seems to grow in that darkness."[26] Hyde solidifies this problem around the issue of usury. To justify the practice against the Gospel prohibition, the Jew is found to be imperfect, to be naturally usurious and so inseparable from this onerous social task.[27] With Luther the split is secured when he accepts usury on civil grounds and rejects it on moral grounds. The Jew who is alien is part of the society that can generate no value. It is necessary but without grace.

This kind of transcendence that requires the negative other in order to define itself is further delineated in the idea of critical reason that comes to characterize the bourgeois relation to the world. Critical reason is the cultural counterpart to religious transcendence, the way to transcend the contingency of the social world. Tillich distinguishes this relation to the world as one that in bourgeois thought is corrective, not normative. It is critical in that it transforms what exists into its own purposes. What it creates as new is in this reconstruction instead of in originality.[28] The activity of the corrective dynamic by which reason brings everything in line with itself is that of splitting, of dissolving, of separating. In the collapse of transcendence with critical reason, transcendence as it applies to this world becomes synonymous with theory, with understanding. To understand is to separate. To think is to conquer. To conquer requires separating oneself as the thinker from the other to be conquered.[29]

Transcending and reasoning then are historically generated as nonsocial activities about society. They are universally available to those who claim to have the capacities to be removed from society. But this is not a mental capacity; it is a social one. The critical transcendence of the bourgeois not only comes from those individuals who by virtue of their autonomy are free to think this way, but it can only be created by such individuals. The contingent disappears in the universal. Essence and manifestation achieve a fit. Others do not fit.

By this account the outer affects the inner for some of us and not for others. Some of us can through our property buy our way out of society, out of otherness. Others are more socially constituted and therefore less capable of reason and transcendence. This notion is stated baldly by Reinhold Niebuhr in *Moral Man and Immoral Society* when he claims that the bourgeois is more of an individual than the proletariat, whose attachment to their collectivity limits their capacity for reason and transcendence.[30]

> The proletarian on the other hand is not enough of an individual, in the attainments of his own cultural life and in the conditions of his social life, to be strongly moved by the canons of individual morality. He is most conscious of the morality of group behavior. He is not only more completely immersed in his own group than the more privileged classes, but he feels the effect of the behavior of other groups upon his life more definitely than do the members of privileged classes.[31]

If society is other then it is "the others" who are society. Society as other than we are is the others as other than we are, as those whom we can describe and for whom we can prescribe. By making society an entity to be avoided, we avoid its reality. We avoid historical dilemmas and contradictions; we avoid reasons that are not our reasons by denying their transcendent value, as in many critiques of liberation theology. We avoid the connections through which the problems are created. We especially avoid this with the language of responsibility, obligation, and compromise, through which we legitimate our moral relationship to an entity, society, that we do not consider moral and to those who by our terms present only imperfect social and philosophical credentials, those flawed in the flow from the inner to the outer self.

But the bourgeois cannot acknowledge that other social and moral worlds exist. To acknowledge that other worlds exist is to place limits on our own. Instead we assign limits to those we define as other and whose morality we presume to be insufficient, founded on necessity, not freedom. From the bourgeois perspective the "morality" of the other is functional and nonsymbolic. It is social and particular. It is manifestation with no essence. No universalizing features inhere in caring for children, cutting sugar cane, or picking grapes. These activities are not the stuff of which theory is made. They are outside criticism, rationality, and transcendence. They are activities of those who embody desire, disorder, bodiliness itself, of those who embody society.

The connection between confronting the reality of society and the reality of otherness is made in the identification of those whose moralities we avoid, those whom we avoid identifying as moral agents. The issue is formally resolved by strategies of extension or inclusion or even difference. But it can be substantively addressed only through the histories of people themselves. The challenge of the moral and social histories of black women, of slave communities, of nonbourgeois women, is not only to reveal agency and thus legitimate "outsiders" to "insiders."[32] The challenge is the presence of other worlds that not only resist bourgeois control but also resist those who speak for them from any perspective under the assumption that they have no voice or world of their own.

The hegemony of liberal moral theory on this count is increasingly well documented, but theories of nondomination and liberation may participate in this problem as well. Axel Honneth argues that Habermas' allegiance to the privileged, public categories of elaborated theories blinds him to the normative codes of suppressed classes.[33] Among the new voices of social and moral theory, feminists are particularly vulnerable to this problem, in part because we have enjoyed some success and in part because women divide sharply in our experiences of otherness, especially by race and class and religion. Feminist theories of mutuality, reciprocity, difference, plurality, and relationality can also reproduce the otherness of domination and lift the burden of otherness from ourselves when we define the conditions of freedom for others. However nondominating we intend these conditions to be, it is we who decided to have this dialogue. We have radically improved its terms. It is inclusive; it is yours. But what are we giving? Is it a gift? Or is it the demand that the stranger either be the alien who needs us or be like us?

My argument does not presume moral heroism for those historically other. Too easily we slip out of the tension of otherness with the assertion or protest of this romantic claim. Nor does my argument presume the demise of all critical standards of reason and responsibility. Likewise we resist confronting otherness by claiming that no criteria of reason or responsibility from which to make moral judgments exist except our own. But bourgeois critical reason can neither complete nor reconstitute itself. Unless we hear the reasons and responsibilities of those historically other, we cannot articulate in theory what is radical in nonbourgeois social experience. To reduce this conflict to that of one-dimensional ideologies and interests undercuts any possibility of seeing the contradictions that other histories reveal; it reiterates a morality whose historical contribution can neither confront nor negate its historical domination. The problem of otherness opens up the moral question of what those with power have done historically to remove the threat of otherness in themselves, to assure that they will never be a stranger, much less an alien, to define the world so that it is theirs and no one else's.

Those historically other are not waiting for the moral codes of the dominant; they bring their own. We have to wonder if our tendered terms of intersubjectivity and reciprocity will meet their criteria. How will their history of reciprocity meet with our theory about a world yet to be made? How will their experiences of being our shadow transform our worlds? Can we be, as Lugones and Spelman ask, "unintrusive, unimportant, patient to the point of tears"? Can we "come to terms with the sense of alienation, of not belonging, of having your own world thoroughly disrupted," criticized by those who are harmed by it and who find fault with concepts we have held to be central?[34]

The hermetically sealed autonomous self removes otherness from itself and takes up a critical stance toward the world, a world which could only gain value as it approximates the freedom of autonomy and loses its identity as world. The autonomous self has no need of the world it criticizes. In this self-sufficiency, the critic of the world has no need for the reasons or principles of others. The critic has no need for humility, because her or his position is complete, without lack. Without lack the self cannot even glimpse the otherness embedded in its historical self-construction; nor can it, for that matter, grasp the otherness necessary for its own becoming. Unless thinkers take seriously the challenges which the bourgeois history of otherness poses to our thought, we will continue to reassert hegemony. Contingency will be cast on the outsider and humility will be again a value we recommend only to others.

NOTES

1. See, for example, Linell E. Cady, "Relational Love: A Feminist Christian Vision," in *Embodied Love: Sensuality and Relationship as Feminist Values*, ed. Paula M. Cooey, Sharon A. Farmer, Mary Ellen Ross (San Francisco: Harper & Row, 1987), pp. 134–49; Drucilla Cornell, "Toward a Modern/Postmodern Reconstruction of Ethics," *University of Pennsylvania Law Review* 133, no. 2 (1985): 291–380; Ruth L. Smith, "Morality and Perceptions of Society: The Limits of Self-Interest," *Journal for the Scientific Study of Religion* 26 (Fall 1987): 279–93; Iris M. Young, "The Ideal of Community and the Politics of Difference," unpublished paper.

2. This connection is discussed by Norman O. Brown, *Life against Death* (Middletown, Conn.: Wesleyan University Press, 1959), chap. 14: "The Protestant Era"; and by Lewis Hyde, *The Gift* (New York: Random House, 1979), chap. 7: "Usury: A History of Gift Exchange."

3. Maria C. Lugones and Elizabeth Spelman, "Have We Got a Theory for You! Feminist Theory, Cultural Imperialism, and the Demand for 'The Woman's Voice,'" *Hypatia*, Special Issue of *Women's Studies International Forum* 6 (1983): 576.

4. Charles H. Long, *Signification: Signs, Symbols, and Images in the Interpretation of Religion* (Philadelphia: Fortress Press, 1986), p. 147.

5. Ibid., p. 150.

6. Ibid.; Ralph Ellison, *Invisible Man* (New York: New American Library, 1947), p. 7.

7. Ernst Troeltsch, "Contingency," *Encyclopedia of Religion and Ethics*, pp. 88–89.

8. Long, *Signification*, p. 162.

9. Jean-Paul Sartre, "Portrait of the Antisemite," in *Existentialism from Dostoyevsky to Sartre*, ed. Walter Kaufmann (New York: Meridian, 1956): 270–87.

10. Significant works in this poststructuralist move include Roland Barthes, *Image-Music-Text*, trans. Stephen Health (New York: Hill & Wang, 1977); and Jacques Derrida, *Speech and Phenomena*, trans. David B. Allison (Evanston, Ill.: Northwestern University Press, 1973); and *Of Grammatology*, trans. Gayatri Chakravorty Spivak (Baltimore: Johns Hopkins University Press, 1974). Mark Taylor develops theological aspects of deconstruction in *Erring* (Chicago: University of Chicago Press, 1984).

11. G. W. F. Hegel, *The Logic*, Part 1 of *The Encyclopedia of the Philosophical Sciences*, trans. William Wallace (Oxford: Clarendon Press, 1975): 165–73.

12. See, for example, Derrida, *Speech and Phenomena*, p. 148.

13. For a critique of the modernist notion of disinterest and the standard of impartiality, see Iris M. Young, "Impartiality and the Civic Public," in *Feminism as Critique*, ed. Seyla Benhabib and Drucilla Cornell (Minneapolis: University of Minnesota Press, 1987), pp. 57–76.

14. Michael Ryan, *Marxism and Deconstruction* (Baltimore: Johns Hopkins University Press, 1982), p. 72.

15. Seyla Benhabib, "The Generalized and the Concrete Other," in *Feminism as Critique*, ed. Benhabib and Cornell, pp. 77–95.

16. For a discussion of this problem in deconstruction see Terry Eagleton, *Literary Theory* (Minneapolis: University of Minnesota Press, 1983), pp. 144–47.

17. Ryan, *Marxism and Deconstruction*, p. 70.

18. Sartre, "Portrait of the Antisemite," p. 287.

19. Lugones and Spelman, "Have We Got a Theory for You!" p. 575.

20. See Smith, "Morality and Perceptions of Society."

21. Roberto Mangabeira Unger, *Knowledge and Politics* (New York: Free Press, 1975), p. 83.

22. Brown, *Life against Death*, p. 211. The strength of the modern dichotomy between self and society can be seen in the theological claims of the Reformation which associate all visible reality, including society, with evil. Brown argues that for Luther society is a macrocosm of "the demonic power of the devil." Luther is relentless in his denunciation: "The world is the devil and the devil is the world. . . . Everything is full of

devils, in the courts of princes, in houses, in fields, in streets, in water, in wood, in fire" (Brown, *Life against Death*, p. 212).

23. Hyde, *The Gift*, p. 116.

24. See, for example, Reinhold Niebuhr, *Moral Man and Immoral Society* (New York: Charles Scribner's Sons, 1932).

25. Unger, *Knowledge and Politics*, p. 160.

26. Hyde, *The Gift*, p. 118.

27. Ibid.

28. Paul Tillich, *The Socialist Decision*, trans. Franklin Sherman (New York: Harper & Row, 1977), p. 54.

29. Feminist theorists have also criticized bourgeois epistemology on this account. See, for example, Sandra Harding and Merrill B. Hintikka, eds., *Discovering Reality* (Dordrecht: D. Reidel Publishing Co., 1983) pp. 225-44.

30. Niebuhr, *Moral Man and Immoral Society*, p. 176.

31. Ibid. It can be argued that this analysis of the proletariat is only one side of Niebuhr's "dialectical approach" and neglects his analysis of the bourgeois. However, while Niebuhr is not uncritical of the limitations of the moral perspective of the middle class, his criticism addresses their attempts to protect their own privilege instead of the nature of their individuality which is presumably untouched by their sociality.

32. See, for example, Kate Canon, "Hitting a Straight Lick with a Crooked Stick: The Womanist Dilemma in the Development of a Black Liberation Ethic," *The Annual of the Society of Christian Ethics* (1987): 165-77; Eugene Genovese, *Roll, Jordan, Roll: The World the Slaves Made* (New York: Vintage, 1976); Ruth L. Smith and Deborah M. Valenze, "Mutuality and Marginality: Liberal Moral Theory and Working-Class Women in Nineteenth-Century England," *Signs* 13 (Winter 1988): 277-98.

33. Axel Honneth, "Moral Consciousness and Class Domination: Some Problems in the Analysis of Hidden Morality," *Praxis International* 2 (April 1982): 12-25.

34. Lugones and Spelman, "Have We Got a Theory for You!" p. 580.

11
Mass Death and Autonomous Selves
EDITH WYSCHOGROD

THE DEATHS OF VAST NUMBERS of persons brought about by human agency is the most significant historical event of our time. This is because if we fail to neutralize or eliminate at least one especially threatening form of mass death, nuclear war, the opportunity to resolve other problems, famine in underdeveloped countries or the AIDS crisis, may never arise. To be sure, developing the means to circumvent nuclear disaster and, by extension, chemical and biological warfare, does not assure progress toward the elimination of hunger or a cure for a fatal disease. Nor can we be certain that these or unforeseen alternative catastrophes might not strike us down first. But it is at least arguable that, among the intractable phenomena mentioned, manmade mass death is of our own making and therefore easier to understand, epistemologically cleaner, and more open to alteration by human agents. The common-sense perception is summarized in Vico's remark in the *New Science* that human history and natural history differ in that we have made the one but not the other. Another way of describing this view is that history is the sphere of human freedom. I define freedom as the ability of an agent to affect some future event or events together with the belief that the agent can bring about the outcome intended. The freedom of agents is altered both by internal and external constraints on his or her action.

I have no quarrel with the common-sense view that it may be possible to avoid nuclear war if appropriate measures are taken. Nor do I think such measures are, as Chernus has argued, either facilitated or forestalled because nuclear weapons have acquired a negative sacrality.[1] Instead, the source of my worry is a theory of the self as independent thinker and actor that is bound up with the common-sense view. The received theory, although widely held, has been significantly modified by farsighted anti-Cartesian philosophers for conceptual reasons, and now, in a manner that remains to be specified, is changing under the impact of mass death. The most recent alterations occurred within the comparatively brief compass of the present century and can conveniently be dated as beginning with World War I and continuing to the present.

In what follows, I show how manmade mass death bears on our views of self, freedom, and moral action. In the first section of this paper, I describe two characteristic forms of manmade mass death, the concentration camp system and nuclear war, together with some difficulties that arise in connection with this account of types. In the second section I turn to some models of the self, first the pattern underlying some earlier conceptions of self held by otherwise different thinkers of the Western philosophical tradition, then a later modification of this design, and finally the sea change in the concept of self that is only now coming into focus as a result of manmade mass death. I show that some redescriptions of agency are suggested by the two manifestations of manmade mass death — the camp system and nuclear war — and that these new views are not only consistent with a changed view of self but inseparable from it. In the third section I consider the consequences for moral action that are bound up with these shifts in self-concepts.

TYPES OF MASS DEATH

Wars and natural calamities have decimated whole populations in the past. What is unprecedented in the phenomenon considered here is that the deaths of millions are the result of a rational calculation of *means*, bureaucratic techniques applied to new technologies. Scale is no longer reckoned by head count alone but in terms of the compressed time frame in which the liquidation of persons occurs. But the phenomenon is only loosely described when these features are attributed to it. Close inspection reveals that humanly contrived mass death characteristically shows itself in two quite different ways. The first is a complex of practices and policies that isolate whole populations, herd them together in enclosures or camps, and consign them to slave labor or extinction *tout court*. The second is nuclear war, to be considered later.

Elsewhere I have referred to the first form as the death-world in order to contrast it with what Edmund Husserl called the life-world—the given, taken-for-granted, everyday natural and social world that is the backdrop for all our activities.[2] Spatial and temporal compression and a foreclosing of future options characterize the death-world. This manifestation of manmade mass death aims at the destruction of a specific group of persons and may occur apart from the context of war. Accused (often falsely) of having aims inimical to the interests of the larger embedding society, a group becomes the negative symbol of such social ideals as the Aryan race, the perfect revolutionary, the spirit of the military junta, white supremacy, and the like. It is cordoned off as tainted, impure, and often also morally corrupt. The phenomena generated by this pattern include not only concentration and extermination camps at the far end of the spectrum but also branch forms of varying degrees of severity. Thus hard labor as a technique for reeducating the urban population in Hungary after the revolution of 1956 can be seen as a branch form when compared with the Draconian measures having an allegedly similar aim pursued by the Khmer Rouge after the occupation of Phnom Penh. There is little disagreement that the full force of what lies at the far end of the spectrum—degradation, death, and human suffering on an unprecedented scale—is signified by the term *Auschwitz*. In the technical sense *Auschwitz* refers to the concentration camp located near Oswiescem. The name *Auschwitz*, however, has come to symbolize the vast Nazi extermination program.

It is neither useless nor unimportant to consider other historical phenomena that belong to the complex of events targeting a specified group within an embedding society. It may be helpful to think of these other events as puzzle cases.[3] In doing so a way is cleared for pondering a whole range of phenomena without prejudicing this special character of *Auschwitz*. The events I shall consider are not puzzling in regard to their morally repugnant character or the human suffering inflicted. But they are enigmatic in another way. They raise questions about whether they are phenomenologically identical, the same in every significant respect — whether, in fact, this can be determined, and, if not, whether one, both, or neither of these events belong to the death-world *unambiguously*. Consider the government-sanctioned disappearance and murder of some nine thousand civilians by the military government of Argentina that came to an end with its fall from power in 1983.[4] Although entailing the death of large numbers of "internal enemies," this event is not Auschwitz, the extreme of the death-world. Is it the same, however, as the detention, torture, and death of blacks in smaller numbers in prison blocks connected with the South African government's apartheid policies? Do both count as death-world events? Is there a point at which the death-world ceases to exist, a border where one case merits inclusion and the other not? It is hard to believe that the difference between inclusion and exclusion could consist in the small differences described between the South African and the Argentinean cases. It is, to borrow a term from Derek Parfit, an empty question. Is Argentina but not South Africa to count as a death-world phenomenon? The claim that South Africa does not but that Argentina does is neither true nor false but indeterminate. We can decide arbitrarily to assign it a place, but doing so in no way changes the description of the events involved. South Africa and Argentina are simply equivalent to the multiple constituent continuities and connections that make up these events. This analysis is useful in the present context because it helps us to grasp the full force and significance of the far end. Auschwitz is the standard of reference for the death-world. There are, however, two undesirable possible outcomes of this claim (a claim I do not dispute) which this analysis helps to defeat. On the one hand, when the uniqueness of Auschwitz is interpreted to mean that nothing else is like Auschwitz, this may have the paradoxical and unintended effect of diminishing rather than increasing its power as a symbol. This view may encourage people to tolerate extreme injustice because such injustice still falls short of Auschwitz. On the other hand, if a large number of intolerable acts are compared to Auschwitz, the enormity of Auschwitz is attenuated or lost. But on the present analysis, Auschwitz remains sui generis, the darkest of dark death-worlds. Other events need not be compared with it. At the same time, they need not be forced into an identity or lack of identity with one another so as to include or exclude them from the death-world. There need be no answer to the questions that try to do this; they are *empty* questions. The South African and Argentine cases simply are what they are made up of, the arrest and deportation of persons, interrogation under torture, and torture *tout court*. Once the question of whether a worrisome case is still part of the death-world is mooted, each event retains its negative moral force. The result is a certain fluidity among puzzle cases but not a diminishing of the moral significance of each. At the same time, the extraordinary character of the sui generis phenomenon at the far end remains. This is important to my argument because I believe that smaller scale cases reinforce the memory of Auschwitz without attenuating its power or having to establish their credentials in its light. Taken together, present-day events and Auschwitz as a living symbol erode our received notions of self and freedom in a manner still to be interpreted.

Consider now the second type of manmade mass death, nuclear war. It does not help any in trying to grasp the impact on our view of self and freedom to think of nuclear war in terms of gradations in which ambiguous cases arise. This is because nuclear war must be viewed as a *total phenomenon* threatening planetary survival. It is generally agreed, as Lord Zuckerman argues:

> There would be no neutrals in a nuclear war. Nuclear explosions have no regard for national boundaries. That was proved by Chernobyl — a relatively minor nuclear accident compared to what the explosion of a nuclear warhead could do. Whereas in the past the destruction caused by war has been suffered only by the contestants, this would no longer be so in a war in which nuclear weapons were used.[5]

Even if (as is highly improbable) this conclusion is wrong, nuclear conflict is never *imagined* as *une petite guerre*. Even survivors of Hiroshima and Nagasaki, the *hibakshi*, who had no foreknowledge of the bomb's power, describe an eschatological and apocalyptic *grande guerre* in which the whole earth seemed to be coming to an end. Unlike the character of the death-world for which ample detail can be supplied, for obvious reasons there could be no experiential account of present-day nuclear war. But even survivors of the earlier bomb reported that they thought of a nuclear world as futureless in the sense that time had run out.[6]

Earlier it was suggested that the camp system and phenomena linked with it are bound up with notions of *taint* and *impurity*. Nuclear war, however, should be interpreted in a different framework, that of military history. The earliest extended accounts of the *ethoi* of war found in various epic traditions stress the virtues of courage and cunning. Achilles and Odysseus taken together constitute the might of the Hellenes. Because they embody the same martial virtues, the sons of Priam were worthy, if less accomplished and less divinely favored, adversaries. Conflict is aimed at settling a dispute and is played out against the backdrop of Olympian politics. Similarly the biblical book of Samuel establishes ancient Israelite martial tradition, especially in its account of the war against the Philistines. David's exploits, bold and tactically astute, are underwritten by a transcendent power. To be sure, what is holy is holy because loved by God, but God's love comes to rest on one already marked by sagacity and daring. The Indian epic tradition, despite the wavering of Arjuna and some fatalistic aspects of the *karma* tradition described in the *Bhagavad Gita*, endorses daring and cunning within the framework of caste and family. Even when Greek and Israelite perspectives are modified by Israelite prophecy and the Gospels, changes later reflected in the just war tradition, the concept of martial virtue is maintained.

This brief historical sketch is intended only to suggest that the earliest accounts of war are bound up with some specific notions of self and freedom. Individuals are the initiators of actions which are aimed at deciding a disputed issue. The constraints on agency are theological, customary, and calculative. The first two types of constraint establish the framework of agency: the leeway sanctioned by divine power in the deployment of force and the limits imposed by social roles. Within these boundaries calculation and cunning are given free rein. Apart from the dispute to be resolved by war, the allowable intentions and practices of adversaries are roughly symmetrical. But later, when hostilities are extended, there is less and less agreement about more and more. The thinning of consensual ties forces adversaries to trade on what each believes is common to all. (Compare Herodotus' account of the Greeks in the war between Athens and Sparta with

Tacitus' view of Roman citizenship in the campaigns against the Armenians or Syrians.) As agreement about self and freedom based on shared folkways diminishes, it is supplanted by a reflective view. Individuals are increasingly defined in terms of a fundament of rationality taken to be normative for thought, utterance, and action.

Beginning with World War I, events occur which change this picture. Wars are still intended to resolve disputes, but the means for waging war conflict with its stated purpose. War's principal aim becomes depriving the enemy of its armies. The destruction of persons depends on sophisticated weapons systems rather than on tactical genius or relationships in the field. In recent wars, visible adversary lines are drawn among recognizable sociopolitical entities that align bureaucratic and technological power. But invisible undeclared lines exist between those who collectively control these technologies and those who lack effective counterforce. Nuclear war obliterates these boundaries as well in that it is more than likely that those who directly control nuclear arsenals, as well as those who do not, will become its victims.[7]

In one important respect the effects on self and freedom of nuclear war and the death-world converge. Human beings naturally anticipate the future. When war, disease, and natural catastrophe strike, hope for species continuity persists. Even millenarian movements, past and present, assume that for the most part a saving remnant will remain and, if not, someone loosely continuous with a preceding self will arise from the ashes. Both the camp system and nuclear war frustrate this natural anticipation, each in a distinctive way. The camp system replicates imagined conditions of negative postmortem survival, an eternal present complete with torturers and fiery furnaces. Inmates experience themselves as the living dead. Hope centers on the unlikely survival of some few who might establish collective continuity, either symbolic or biological. In the event of full-scale nuclear war such hopes would lack all plausibility. It can be argued that, so long as it is not in any individual's power to prevent nuclear war, perhaps it is better simply to live in the present and so avoid the anxiety of anticipation. If worry about the future ceases, concern for one's own death which cannot be avoided in any case would also fall away.[8] Not only does this argument issue from a misunderstanding about the future-directed aims of present action; it also encourages despair and inhibits constructive response. Because the death-world and nuclear war maintain these negative tendencies come what may, they already play an important part in altering our self-concepts and the uses we make of them. Consider the case in Garrison Keillor's fictional account of the young girl about to be confirmed in the Lutheran Church. "She turned on the TV and lost her faith. Men in khaki suits were beating people senseless, shooting them with machine guns, throwing the bodies out of helicopters . . . and she thought, 'This could happen here.'"[9]

THE STRUCTURE OF SELVES

Accounts of the self in its life circumstances, in the present context those of ancient and modern wars and the death-world, are bound up with the general features attributed to selves by philosophers. Only by observing our everyday comportments can the structure of selves be brought to light. There is widespread agreement about the connectedness of the self in action and the self under philosophical scrutiny even among philosophers who agree about little else. Heidegger's account of the *Dasein*, the existing human being, stands or falls on the notion that its way of being can only be brought out by exhibiting it "in its average everydayness [*Alltäglichkeit*]" as it is first encountered in primordial experiences of the world, time, language, and other persons.[10] Similarly Bernard Williams claims, in the spirit of Wittgenstein, that "how truthfulness to an existing self or society is to be combined with reflection" cannot be explained in the formulations of ethical theorists. Instead such a question might be answered through "reflective living [but not] in the way that [ethical theorists] require an answer, as a piece of philosophy. To suppose that, if their formulations are rejected, we are left with *nothing* is to take a strange view of what in social and personal life counts as something."[11]

The term *self* has fallen into philosophical disrepute because it has often been interpreted substantively as an entity alongside of the thoughts, intentions, desires, habits, and actions that, taken together, make up a unified stream of experience. Despite important differences in Plato, Descartes, Kant, and others, this interpretation of the self as thinglike is entrenched in the history of philosophy. The self is seen as the subject of cognitive, productive, and moral acts. For some philosophers — Locke is an example — the self is said to be the same when the same body accompanies a stream of mental acts unified by memory. For others like Plato, the self's identity is strongest when memory, not of experienced facts but of rational principles alone, perdures in the absence of the body. On both interpretations the self initiates its social relations but is prior to them and can exist apart from them. Hegel, despite the difficulties attached to his philosophy of the Absolute, recognized that consciousness of self arises through the connectedness of selves with one another. The self becomes aware of itself when it learns that it is the object of another's experience. Selves are simply the rich network of social relations in which they engage.

But if selves are relational in the sense described, the boundedness, the individuality, of selves is undermined. Recognizing this difficulty, Heidegger argues that what makes selves individuals is the relation of each self to its own death. I cannot substitute my death for that of another nor can another substitute for mine. I can sacrifice my life for another, but this only buys time. On this view, the self is bound up with body, for even if something outlasts the body, the body must certainly come to an end. To be sure, some philosophers have recently begun to imagine how various techniques that would insure bodily continuity, such as cloning, memory cell transplants, and the like would affect the way we think about whether or not one is the same person. Such strategies may be useful when considering formal questions connected with personal identity but have little bearing on the actualities of the death-world. Those who have survived a death-world event and who say that they are no longer the same connect this claim not with bizarre bodily alterations they may have undergone but with the damaged health and psychological changes their suffering has caused.

In the context of the death-world the body takes on significance in another way. Not only does it become the actual object of violence, but it becomes the symbol for vulnerability to violence.[12] The body also acquires meanings that generally are attached to objects of use. Whereas in everyday life tools are extensions of the body, in the death-world the body again becomes an actual or symbolic tool. In the absence even of the simplest equipment, the hand can both become and symbolize a hammer, the torso and limbs a cart, and the like. At the same time the corporeal aspect of selves should not obscure the self as a transactional network of social relations.

It can be argued against the account of a transactional social self that thoughts, beliefs, intentions, and desires are private. Unless I express what I think or inadvertently give myself away through gestures or slips of the tongue, other persons have no access to my experiences. Even when I speak or gesture, my silent thoughts remain private. There is no denying that others cannot gain direct access to my stream of experience, but this is not a definitive argument against the transactional view. Although there is a stream which remains private, available to me alone, the self to whom the stream is open must be constituted first. Were there no awareness of the stream, there would be nothing for the flow of experiences to relate itself to. This self assumes the standpoint of another to the ongoing rush of experiences. But to be other than another presupposes standing apart in social existence from the start.[13]

It may be useful to use the pronouns *I* and *me* to distinguish functionally awareness of the stream from the stream itself, so long as the *I* is not interpreted as thinglike, a position criticized earlier. The *I* is not something timeless but flashes by to join the *me* and thus to become integrated into the stream. In turn, the flux of experience is always in the process of moving into the past. The *me* grows, lengthening as first person flash points are integrated into the past. The content of the *me* can be communicated to others through language.

It may seem as if the body belongs to the *me* because it is something tangible. This is only partly true. There is an aspect of the body that never becomes objective, because it is through the body—its orientation in space and time, the positioning of the sense organs, the organs themselves—that persons and objects communicate themselves to me. The ensemble of *I* and *me* relate harmoniously as long as the self's transactions with its social and physical world allow it to affect further events. Thus its sphere of freedom as defined earlier is intact although its freedom may vary in degree. But in the death-world physical conditions hostile to life and psychological degradation work together to force an identification by victims with those already dead. In the case of nuclear war, however, human extinction as a result of human acts is envisioned as possible or even likely. For those who have not survived a death-world or the use of nuclear weapons, the two work together to form a background of morbidity against which other experiences are played off. The result is the deterioration of the active *I* with an attendant loss of the self's robustness. This decline of the *I* means not that people are inactive but that the self's relations to the future have been impaired.

BOUNDLESS AND BOUNDED ALTRUISM

While nuclear war and the death-world reinforce the background belief that there will be no future, some distinctions may help clarify the relation to the future of each of these phenomena. For victims of the death-world, projection into both the near and the distant future is curtailed. Because immediate hardship overrides other concerns, there is little thought about the far future except for the often feeble hope that at least some will survive. For those few who emerge alive, wishes bound up with the future come into conflict. On the one hand, survivors believe they should recount their experiences as a way of honoring the dead and warning the living about a possible recurrence of past events. This entails projecting into the far future. A Tibetan monk interviewed at Drepung reports, "I spent 21 years in prison. . . . I know what electric shocks are like. . . . We say if you kill us, the Dalai Lama is still alive."[14] But after release from the death-world, the survivor encounters the nuclear fears common to all. Whatever he or she may believe about future lives, a Tibetan Buddhist who has experienced the deaths of large numbers of other Tibetans faces the general threat of nuclear annihilation. All who are now alive are threatened, so that vast numbers of people share this fear in varying degrees.

The fear of death and the desire to remain alive are not new. Aristotle and Spinoza thought the desire for self-preservation was an expression of a living thing's essence. Hobbes made it the foundation of his ethical system while Nietzsche and Schopenhauer attributed cosmic power to the will to live. For the most part these earlier views took for granted that the natural outcome of the desire for self-preservation is an ethic of self-interest. Nuclear fear for the future reinforced by the death-world's impact on the self does not do away with the desire to remain alive. Instead it overturns the self-interest interpretation of the will to live.

Because the transactional self described earlier is already social, the desire to persevere in one's existence includes other people—if not directly, at least indirectly. The wish for self-preservation under ordinary circumstances encompasses the hope for the continuation of one's social world as well as for oneself since the self as social and transactional is a collective term. In the context of nuclear war, the self so threatened has become a *we* that includes everyone without exception who is now alive as well as future generations. The proposition "I want to remain alive in the nuclear age" cannot be strictly interpreted to mean "I want to survive together with my family." Because the threat of total nuclear war exempts no one, the demand to remain alive must include this newly introjected collective whole. The result is that I am required to consider the fate not only of others to whom I have emotional or prudential attachments, but of all others. The result is that in committing myself to anyone's survival in the context of full-scale nuclear war I am obliged to commit myself to furthering everyone's survival.

Dostoyevsky in *The Brothers Karamazov* makes this point with his parable of the onion. A wicked peasant woman dies leaving no good deeds behind her. When she is plunged into the lake of fire, her guardian angel reminds God that once she gave a beggar woman an onion. God tells the angel to let her grasp the onion and be pulled out on the condition that the onion does not break. Just as the angel is about to succeed, one of the other sinners notices that she is being rescued. They catch hold of her but she hurls them back. "I'm to be pulled out and not you. It's my onion, not yours," she cries. With this, the onion breaks and she is hurled back into the burning lake.[15]

Paradoxically, in the context of nuclear war the very reason for commitment to the whole human community—its possible destruction—is a key factor in creating the backdrop of morbidity, despair, and hopelessness. But an important change has occurred.

Once the self-preservation demand has become other-inclusive, selves are in transition from psychological to ethical selves. This does not assure the ability to withstand the pressure of manmade mass death, especially in the light of the diminished force of the *I*. But the self-emptying that decreases the *I*'s power may have two quite different consequences. On the one hand, without the harmonious balance of *I* and *me* of a more robust self, people may continue to pursue private pleasure, where this is politically and socially feasible; and where it is not they may simply surrender to crushing pressures. In fact, these are the responses of most. The effect of the diminished power of the *I* may result in depersonalization, a privation of the force to initiate activity. On the other hand, it may alter self-concepts so that impersonality, a detached objectivity that permits the destitution or need of the other to come to the fore, may motivate one's own acts. Person predicates are translated into impersonal terms.[16] Such a change is anticipated in the Buddhist view that person predicates are harmful because they reinforce egoism and selfishness. A loosening of this language could have the effect of encouraging benevolence and self-sacrifice.

It is useful in pursuing this point further to consider again the distinction between nuclear war and the death-world. In the context of the death-world, resistance to it from within is nearly impossible, since even extreme acts of sacrifice such as the willingness to surrender one's life for another have little hope for success. In that context acts of generosity such as giving up food or equipment, or willingness when possible to substitute oneself for others when "punishments" are being meted out, count as acts of extreme unselfishness. The scope of the self's freedom is, however, radically curtailed in that victims can hardly affect future events. Because room for action is close to the null point, the amount of effort required on the part of individuals to have an effect is inversely proportional to the rigidity of the system. Still, the destitution of others may motivate acts of extraordinary self-sacrifice. Such acts may miscarry, but, if their intent is understood, they can have paradigmatic force. An example is giving away food to save a life although the victim dies anyway. Some acts that appear selfish, such as staying alive under odious circumstances, may actually be altruistic if they are intended to bring these circumstances to light later. This is because successful acts may be measured not in terms of immediate success but in terms of consequences for a more remote future. Franz Jagerstatter, a German Catholic peasant who refused to be conscripted into the German army during the Nazi period because he believed the war to be unjust, had no effect on the war's outcome, but his act affected the postwar self-evaluation of some German Roman Catholics.[17] The opportunity to act occurred, however, because his freedom was only partially curtailed. Quixotic acts, striking out wildly in a fashion that may unnecessarily injure others, are not exemplary. But in actual situations it is not easy to tell whether acts claimed to be absurd and useless are genuinely so or whether the claim itself reflects a disguised reluctance to act.

The important point is that when the sphere of freedom is radically curtailed, boundless altruism is desirable but is rarely feasible. It does not follow that the right to persevere in existence *excludes* oneself. It cannot become mandatory that one sacrifice one's life. But when the *I* self is transformed into an impersonal, but not depersonalized, self, exceptional individuals may be moved to boundless altruism by the extreme distress of others. Because the simplest altruistic acts are often punished with death, when such acts occur they may become boundlessly altruistic. The impact of such acts may alleviate immediate distress, but on the other hand they may become paradigmatic only in the future.

When egocentrism diminishes in the death-world, the other's suffering is brought to light in a new way, as soliciting benevolence. The other's need does not appeal to sympathy and compassion, because these emotions begin with the self as their affective center and radiate toward the other. As such they cannot provide a starting point for altruism. Instead, the other's plight appears as a language-like appeal in the imperative voice. The other's destitution is not given in the form "X is destitute," but rather as "You *must* help X because she is destitute."[18]

In the case of nuclear war no appeal issues from another to the self. One problem bound up with nuclear threat is our difficulty in picturing it. By touching everyone's life it appears to touch no one's. Individual action to thwart nuclear destruction seems useless. Although the sphere of freedom is far larger than in the death-world, the effect of any one person's efforts is unnoticeable, and individual efforts that are conspicuous may seem quixotic, such as the protest of Matthias Rust, the young West German pilot who landed his small plane on Red Square as a peace protest. The relative ineffectiveness of individual action does not rule out the possibility that large numbers of persons acting in concert might produce perceptible change. However, it can also be argued that, because nuclear arsenals are in the hands of governments, even collective action may prove futile. But governments are made up of social transactional selves and so are not immune to influence. In any event, the threat is sufficiently great to make taking steps worthwhile.

My reason for pursuing the point about collective action is not to advocate any specific course of policy but to provide a backdrop for seeing an important difference between the death-world and nuclear threat as this difference bears on the problem of altruistic action. Boundless altruism, which I link to the death-world, is, odd as it may seem, structurally closer to egoism than to bounded altruism because it presupposes an asymmetry between self and other. The egoist places self-interest ahead of others' interests; the boundless altruist, others' interests before those of self. Bounded altruism, which I link to nuclear war, is based on the parity of selves impersonally considered. Individual action is undertaken in the interest of the human community as a whole rather than in response to the distress of extreme situations.

CONCLUSIONS

Twentieth-century manmade mass death falls into two distinctive categories: the death-world and nuclear war. The first is made up of enclaves in which large numbers of persons are subjected to physical and psychological suffering and death. Auschwitz is the extreme case, but the status of other morally repugnant cases must be considered. Both the death-world and nuclear war reinforce one another in diminishing the self's capacity for spontaneous action. Depersonalization and diminished effectiveness in the face of pandemic death are the result. But freedom, an agent's capacity to affect future events, requires separate analysis in each context. In the death-world exceptional individuals may not suffer depersonalization. Instead, egolessness may take the form of impersonality that, together with minimally enabling circumstances, may allow the agent to put aside selfish claims and act with boundless altruism. Such individuals interpret another's destitution as a moral claim for which they are answerable. Indicative statements about the suffering of others are taken as imperatives demanding moral responses. Restrictions on freedom, however, make all action perilous.

The threat of nuclear war affects all persons alive as well as future generations. Even if the sphere of freedom in which action is possible is enlarged, the effect that any one person's actions can have is limited. Under these circumstances, limited benevolence is called for. This follows from the claim that a transactional social self which desires to persevere in existence includes a relational field of others in its wish. Once the whole human community is threatened, the self must wish for the survival of everyone in wishing for the preservation of a few.

NOTES

1. Ira Chernus, *Dr. Strangegod: On the Symbolic Meaning of Nuclear Weapons* (Charleston, S.C.: University of South Carolina Press, 1985).

2. Edmund Husserl, *The Crisis of European Sciences and Transcendental Phenomenology*, trans. David Carr (Evanston, Ill.: Northwestern University Press, 1970), pp. 142–43.

3. The notion of *puzzle cases* is developed in Derek Parfit, *Reasons and Persons* (Oxford: Oxford University Press, 1986), pp. 213, 239.

4. Figures cited are from "The Pope and the Victims," *Topics of the Times, New York Times*, 15 April 1987.

5. Lord Solly Zuckerman, "The Nuclear Hope," *New York Review of Books*, 7 May 1987, p. 44.

6. Robert J. Lifton, *Death in Life: Survivors of Hiroshima* (New York: Basic Books, 1982), esp. chap. 1.

7. For a more extended analysis of this point see Edith Wyschogrod, *Spirit in Ashes: Hegel, Heidegger, and Man-Made Mass Death* (New Haven, Conn.: Yale University Press, 1985), pp. 52–57.

8. In support of the position that worry about the future is undesirable see Parfit, *Reasons and Persons*, pp. 174–77.

9. Garrison Keillor, *Leaving Home* (New York: Viking Press, 1987), p. 234.

10. Martin Heidegger, *Being and Time*, trans. John Macquarrie and Edward Robinson (New York: Harper & Row, 1962), 370, p. 421.

11. Bernard Williams, *Ethics and the Limits of Philosophy* (Cambridge, Mass.: Harvard University Press, 1985), p. 200.

12. For an analysis of the symbolic significance of torture see Elaine Scarry, *The Making and Unmaking of the World* (New York: Oxford University Press, 1985).

13. For an analysis of the self along comparable lines see George Herbert Mead, *On Social Psychology: Selected Papers*, ed. Anselm Strauss (Chicago: University of Chicago Press, 1964), pp. 242ff.

14. Edward Gargan, "In a Silent Monastery: God, Tears, and Fears," *New York Times*, 6 October 1987.

15. Fyodor Dostoyevsky, *The Brothers Karamazov*, trans. Constance Garnett (New York: Random House, n.d.), pp. 369–70.

16. Thomas Nagel, *The Possibility of Altruism* (Princeton, N.J.: Princeton University Press, 1986), p. 281. See also Parfit, *Reasons and Persons*, p. 225.

17. Jagerstatter's life is the subject of Gordon Zahn, *In Solitary Witness: The Life and Death of Franz Jagerstatter* (London: Geoffrey Chapman, 1966).

18. Emmanuel Levinas makes this point the centerpiece of his ethical metaphysics. See especially *Totality and Infinity*, trans. Alphonso Lingis (Pittsburgh: Duquesne University Press, 1969).

Author Index

Abelard, 51
Aquinas, St. Thomas, 46, 56–57, 111, 119–20, 145–46, 152
Arendt, Hannah, 129–31
Aristotle, 8–10, 111–12, 119, 143–48, 150, 190
Auden, W. H., 160
Augustine, 8, 46, 51, 115

Badari, 137
Barker, Ernest, 147–48, 154
Barth, Karl, 47, 51
Bergmann, Frithjof, 6–7, 11, 96–107
Bergson, Henri, 80–81
Bernard of Clairvaux, 51
Brecht, Bertold, 108
Bultmann, Rudolf, 47, 51

Calvin, John, 46–47, 108
Campanella, Thomas, 8, 111, 117–23
Cavell, Stanley, 18, 20
Cobb, John B., Jr., 47
Colombe, Lodovico delle, 112–13
Croce, Benedetto, 143–44
Curran, Charles, 124

Derrida, Jacques, 168
Descartes, René, 15, 18, 83–84, 187

Dostoevsky, Fyodor, 191
Draper, John W., 108
Dupré, Louis, 9–10, 143–62

Eckhart, 56–57
Ellison, Ralph, 165
Erasmus, 46, 51, 58

Feuerbach, Ludwig, 19, 22
Freud, Sigmund, 4, 47–48, 53–56, 58

Galilei, Galileo, 7–8, 108–25
Gerrish, Brian, 46
Gross, Johannes, 30
Gutierrez, Gustavo, 47

Hampshire, Stuart, 144
Hare, R. M., 144
Hegel, G. W. F., 20, 56–57, 98, 100–101, 130–31, 135, 138, 156–57, 169, 188
Heidegger, Martin, 11, 56–57, 187–88
Hobbes, Thomas, 60, 150–51, 154–55, 171, 190
Horkheimer, Max, 17–19, 26
Hume, David, 84–85, 153
Hyde, Lewis, 172–73

Jaimini, 137
James, William, 16, 18, 24, 81, 84–86, 88
Julian of Norwich, 26

Kant, Immanuel, 37, 39, 79–80, 82–83, 135, 138, 140, 153, 187
Keillor, Garrison, 187
Kierkegaard, Søren, 40
King, Martin Luther, Jr., 70
Koestler, Arthur, 109
Küng, Hans, 124

Lacan, Jacques, 4, 47–48, 53, 56–58
Langford, James R., 7–8, 108–25
Lash, Nicholas, 2–4, 15–29
Lessing, Gotthold, 39
Levi-Strauss, Claude, 56
Lewis, H. D., 84
Locke, John, 60, 152–55, 188
Lonergan, Bernard, 46
Long, Charles, 165, 167
Lugones, Maria, 164–65, 169–70, 176
Luther, Martin, 31–32, 34–36, 40, 46–47, 51, 58, 93–95, 108, 110, 149, 171, 173

Machiavelli, Niccolo, 143–44
Marx, Karl, 16, 18–19, 25, 102, 156–57
Melanchthon, 108
Metz, J. B., 47, 52
Mohanty, J. N., 8–9, 126–40
Moltmann, Jürgen, 3–4, 30–45, 47

Nagel, Thomas, 144
Narada, 135, 137
Neville, Robert, 5, 9, 47, 59–76
Niebuhr, H. Richard, 50
Niebuhr, Reinhold, 171–72, 174
Nielsen, Kai, 20
Nietzsche, Friedrich, 17, 19–20, 190–91

Ogden, Schubert, 47, 51

Peirce, C. S., 80–82
Plato, 10, 146–47, 187–88

Rahner, Karl, 22, 46, 51
Rawls, John, 60, 144, 153
Redondi, Pietro, 109
Rorty, Richard, 19
Rousseau, Jean-Jacques, 98, 151, 154–55
Royce, Josiah, 85–86, 91
Ruether, Rosemary Radford, 47
Russell, Bertrand, 85
Ryan, Michael, 169–70

Santillana, Georgio de, 108–9
Sartre, Jean-Paul, 16–18, 85–86, 167, 169–70
Schopenhauer, Arthur, 190–91
Sengupta, D. S., 135
Siromani, Raghunatha, 136
Smith, Adam, 152–53, 157
Smith, John E., 5–6, 8, 11, 79–95
Smith, Ruth L., 10–11, 163–79
Sölle, Dorothee, 47
Spellman, Elizabeth, 164–65, 170–71
Spinoza, Benedict, 92, 190
Suarez, Francisco, 150, 158–59

Tillich, Paul, 86
Tracy, David W., 4, 11, 46–58
Troeltsch, Ernst, 149, 167

Unger, Roberto, 171, 173

Vacaspati, 128

White, Andrew Dickson, 108
Whitehead, Alfred North, 81–82
Wyschogrod, Edith, 11, 180–96

Subject Index

abortion, 1
adulthood, 2-3, 18, 20, 21, 24
altruism, 190, 192-95
Antigone, 93, 94-95, 130
anti-Semitism, 170, 173
Argentina, 183-84
Auschwitz, 182-84, 194

Bhagavad Gita, 185
Bible, 8, 31, 34, 113-24
Buddhist thought, 9, 56, 137

Calvinism, 35
Catholic theology, 4, 8, 46, 47, 108
Chernobyl, 184
common good, 143, 144-45
community, 2, 3, 4, 5, 9, 11, 12, 21, 25, 144-49, 172, 191, 194-95
concentration camps, 181-82, 185-86
conservatism, 7, 103-6
Copernican system, 108-25
Council of Trent, 110-11, 115
Counter-Reformation, 110
creation, 24

death-world, 11, 180-96
determinism, 9, 79-81, 133-34
dharma, 9, 132, 135-40

economics, 10, 104-6, 152, 156-59, 166-67, 171
ecumenism, 3-4, 30-31, 36, 41-45
Enlightenment, 3, 15, 30, 37-40

feminism, 2
feminist theologies, 47, 51, 53
feminist theory, 164, 169, 175-76

grace of God, 22, 24, 31-33, 46, 51

Hebrew Scripture, 53-54
Hindu thought, 8-9
Hiroshima, 184
hope, 22, 27, 186, 190
hopelessness, 191

idolatry, 21-22
Indian philosophy, 8-9, 126-40

justice, 21, 33, 144-47
justification by faith, 31-33, 35, 36

karma, 9, 131-34

liberalism, 1, 2, 5, 7, 10, 59-61, 64, 67, 71, 74, 103, 163-72, 175

liberation theologies, 8, 47, 51, 52, 53, 174
Lutheranism, 35

mokṣa, 9, 138–39
mystical language, 4, 26–27, 53, 55–58

Nagasaki, 184
natural law, 143
Neoplatonism, 2, 53, 56
New Testament, 49–53
nuclear war, 11, 180–96

prophetic language, 4, 53–58
Protestant theology, 4, 47
Protestantism, 3, 30–45, 110
psychology, 47–48, 53–58
Ptolemaic astronomy, 112
Puritan thought, 5, 59–76

Reformation, 30–35, 110
Renaissance, 110, 111
responsibility, 59–76

Roman Catholicism, 30, 34, 38, 42, 43

Scholasticism, 143, 144, 145, 149, 152
secular world, 35, 36
secularism, 2–3, 18–20
self, 2, 4, 6, 10–11, 12, 46–58, 79–95, 163–66, 168–72, 177, 181, 187–95
self-preservation, 16–18, 190–92, 195
self-sacrifice, 13, 19, 20, 192
Socrates, 93–94, 95, 146
South Africa, 183–84
Stoicism, 143, 148–49, 158
subjectivity, 167–68, 169

truth, 39, 40, 43, 99

virtue, 144–45, 147
vocation, 35

world hunger, 1, 25, 61, 180
worship, 21–22, 38

www.ingramcontent.com/pod-product-compliance
Lightning Source LLC
Chambersburg PA
CBHW030343240426
43661CB00052B/1726